AB ENTERPRISE INC.

The Queendom Diaries

"Pages from the diary of a Queen"

Compiled by Best-Selling Author

Angela N. Brand

Foreword by Veronica Montgomery

An Imprint of AB Enterprise, Inc.

The Queendom Diaries: Pages from the diary of a Queen.

FIRST EDITION

Published by AB Enterprise, Inc.

ISBN: 978-1725053731

ISBN-10:172505373X

DISCLAIMER AND LIMITED LIABILITY:

Dedication

This book is dedicated to all young girls, teenagers, young ladies and women across the globe who have experienced molestation, rape, child abuse, emotional abuse, mental abuse, heartbreaks, divorce or setbacks in their lives. We wrote these letters with the intent to bring enlightenment, inspiration, and empowerment. We understand life brings trials and tribulations, but through these letters we hope to lift burdens and break barriers that have been holding you back.

I also dedicate this book to each author's daughter, granddaughter, and great-granddaughters for generations to come. These letters leave a legacy of wisdom and knowledge in its pages and spirit.

A special thanks and appreciation to my 3 children Jacari, Jafara, and Jazar, they endured some hard times with me and went without because of what I went through. For that I leave the legacy of wisdom and wealth for generations to come that they can be proud of.

I thank my mother Stella Buchanan for the love and support she gives me unselfishly, for all the sacrifices and hard decisions in raising me. Mother I love you and cherish you.

Table of Contents

Foreword

I count it among one of the greatest privileges of life to prepare the foreword for this amazing vehicle of healing and restoration for hurting souls everywhere. I first met Coach AB in 2011, and she's been deep in my heart ever since. She has inspired me, encouraged me, showed tenacity and hunger for purpose from Day 1 and this book is no exception. I've witnessed her triumph over hardship and take deep dives into her soul. I've seen her go where only the bravest souls dare trod within her psyche and from such journeys, she brings forth this jewel of wisdom.

It is a chronicle of her awe-inspiring life journey that is sure to touch women at every age and every stage. Her knack for self-expression, compassion for people and captivating story-telling combined with her rich spiritual sense of healing and peace, makes for a read that cannot be forgotten. I would keep this book as a point of reference, an example, of how to process emotions in a way that leads to wholeness and a more abundant life. I have supreme confidence that this book will reach the masses, but more importantly, it is a life changing read that you can't get in your everyday self-help book.

Most people want to heal on a deep emotional level but are unsure how. This book is the map, the guide, the example. I am so unbelievably happy for you!!

Your friend forever,
Coach Veronica Montgomery

About this Book

This book is a collection of letters from women who want to leave a legacy to inspire women that will walk in their footsteps of life. Each woman puts their heart and soul in this book, to give you a peek into their lives, with the hopes of you reaching your Victory in their story. I personally have been encouraged and healed by the letters of each woman. My prayer is that you see yourself and reflect on your life, and how you can learn and grow from our story. In each letter you will find:

1. Inspiration to reflect within
2. Motivation to move past the hurt and pain that's been holding you in bondage to your past
3. Prayers that were used to release fear and past hurts
4. Personal stories of VICTORY and TRIUMPH
5. The Lessons we learned from the situations we been in
6. Hope that things does get better and turn around in your favor

Introduction

Embrace the Mess, so you can move on and give your Message
-Angela N. Brand

Many of you who are reading this book have things in your life that you regret and wish you could do it all over again. Sometimes thinking to yourself, why did I do that, or how did I get into the relationships that ended with me being hurt and disappointed? And that's ok, this book is filled with those very same thoughts of women who decided not to be selfish and give you their diary of stories and situations they have been in, that could encourage you to pick yourself back up and live again.

While reading this book, please have a box of tissue, a towel or something to wipe your tears. You will be inspired to live again, hope again and believe in yourself again. We allow you into our personal space to share our truth with you. For many of you who will read this book, you may find yourself in, been in, or coming out, of some of the same things each author has experienced, please be open to the possible outcome, and find the answers you need to be set free from the old pain you may be holding on to. So, get your coffee, quiet the kids, close your door, get in your comfortable chair or snuggle in your bed with those rollers in your hair, and enjoy this anthology in the spirit in which it was written in. *Come, let's journey together.*

Diary 1
My Journey to Living the Queendom Life
Author /Compiler-Angela N. Brand

Letter 1: Shattered Dreams

When you put your dreams in the hand of the Lord, they will always manifest.
-Angela N. Brand

Dear Dreamer,

You are like every other young girl with their heads in the clouds, in fairytale land, dreaming of being married, meeting this prince charming husband, and living happily ever after; till death do you part. You wanted the beautiful white wedding dress, with the perfect husband all in your head; you even had the house that sits on the hill with the white picket fence and yes, the dog too. You were sold on the American dream; as an innocent little girl, your hopes and dreams are filled with laughter and joy. Angela, the problem is that it does not exist.

One day, this fairytale life will be shattered by reality; no ideal life or perfect husband, no white dress with a long train, no house with the picket fence, not even a dog. Your reality was that you are being stripped of your innocence, being introduced to sex in a perverse way, starting at the age of 5 years old. During this time, you should have been just worrying about going outside with the other kids; instead you were being filled up by men, making you hold things you can't pronounce. You now had to wonder who was going to come into the bathroom this time and rub their manhood on your *cat*, or who was going to climb on top of you while you slept and put spit on you down there because you were too young to produce moisture for him to try and put his *thing* in you, and rub on your private part.

They told you that you're beautiful and offered you money to do things a little girl should not know how to do, and told you not to tell anyone, that this would be our little secret. As they touched you in places untold, your juices begin to flow. In your mind you are wondering, "What's going on, what is this feeling, I have never felt this before." Little Angela, you are feeling things only adults should feel, but your body is now doing its own thing. After a while, you stopped fighting and gave in, because the strength of this man was too great for you to fight.

So, as you lay there in tears, growing into this woman, but your inner being is still a little child. "Mooooommie where are you, Daaaaaddy I can't find you, why, why did you leave me, why are they doing this to me, what are they doing to me, I don't know what this is?" you screamed and cried deep within yourself, but no one came to your rescue. No one heard you; if only your father was there to protect you and teach you how a man is supposed to treat a woman, maybe this would not have happened. All you got was a dad with his own family; leaving you to fend for yourself, trapped in a child's body doing grown women stuff.

As a little girl you should have been focusing on playing with dolls and doing little girl things, depending on mom and dad to protect and provide for you. Your perception was distorted by someone else's nightmare. Now you hear voices calling your name, tormenting you at night.

You are having thoughts of perverse things, as you touched yourself in strange places. This little girl no longer plays with dolls, no, now she has bigger things to hold. You had men who took your innocence to prove their manhood. As you stayed in silent fear, not knowing how to tell someone what happened to you, you now began to go along with the plan. Instead of dreaming good dreams, you are now having nightmares of your future, not knowing if you will ever find a man to truly love and accept you for you.

This fairytale life is not going as planned; no more hopes, no more dreams, they are all replaced with lies and deceit. The future was a place you once hoped for, now you want it all to end, at the age of 16 you took a knife and started to cut your waist, but because the pain was so great, you could not go through with it. Your aunt Cheryl was your safety net and a place of comfort; she would encourage you on the phone, and talk you out of killing yourself. She knew what you were going through because it happened to her. She would even protect you from one of them, so he wouldn't get to you, like he did the others. Growing up in your family wasn't easy, because there were multiple men touching on you and looking at your body as if you were a grown woman. So now your perception of family and marriage was distorted.

Sweetheart, it was not your fault, you did nothing wrong to deserve this. Rest your soul, everything turns out fine. I learned to protect and comfort you; I learned to put you first. You struggled and had so many heartbreaks along the way, but you embraced your femininity and became open and loving.

Your shattered dreams were put back together like a puzzle and became stronger than ever before. Each part of that puzzle fit right in God's plan for your life. In fact, God gave you better dreams that led you to your purpose and destiny. Angela, no more shattered dreams, no more broken places, no more suffering in silence, they all were replaced by hopes of an expected end that put you on a path to help restore the dreams of other young dreamers.

Psalms of a Dreamer

Oh Lord, my heart hurts, I am but a child, why is this happening to me? You promised to protect and guide me. I cried with a loud cry, but you did not answer me, Lord please hear me. My heart hurts and no one cares. My innocence is gone, and I feel alone, no one hears me crying at night, I'm being touched in places I cannot spell. My dreams are shattered, and I have no hope for the future. Lord, please make this go away and restore my dreams.

~Queen AB

Letter 2: The Search Begin

The True Search is never outside one's self, but searching within
brings the real change.
-Angela N. Brand

Dear Nikki,

As life continued, you began a search to find him. You had no clue of
what you will get yourself into as you go from man to man, club to club,
trying to fill an empty void your father left in you. I know you are hurt
because the last conversation with your dad left you deeply wounded.

After his wife found out about you, your dad called to say you
should never go back to your sibling's house ever again. He didn't ask
how you were doing; he just tried to cover his own ass. This is the time
when rejection sets in like water sets in a bottle. This search continues
until you are forty-two years old, and you found out the dreadful news;
your father had died, and they didn't want you to come to the funeral.
You had to accept the hard-core reality, that you will never have that
relationship with him. Not realizing the love you are searching for was
already locked up inside of you, that it was never lost, it was just
misplaced.

You were so gone from the search, you would think you'd run
into him in public places. The dreams were so real that you thought you
were spending time with him playing in the park. The vivid pictures in
your head kept you hoping, wishing, praying that one day he would call

you to say, "little girl, I love you, I'm sorry, I am so proud of you. I want you in my life; I want to build a relationship with you". You wanted that validation from your dad so bad that you craved it, you searched for it in other people, you ate for it, you drank for it, and you sexed for it, dance for dollars for it, and yes tried to sell your body for it. When in fact, the little girl inside you wanted you to accept her, love her, nurture her, hear her crying inside you, and listen to her. You were so caught up in the rejection that you rejected yourself and your greatness, not seeing the beauty God created in you.

Nikki let me tell you, by the time you get to where I am now, you have received your inner healing, still taking it day by day, step by step and yes, it was a process, but you went through it, you grew through it, you learned through it, and yes you overcame it. You "Took Ownership" and become responsible, dedicated and committed to your personal growth and development. Instead of searching outside yourself, you now search within, knowing you are everything you need to be, proving nothing to no one. You became your validator, your affirmer and your own highest authority. You have mastered the act of being you and have stepped out of the way; I am so proud of the woman you have become, understanding that the search started and ended with you.

Psalms of a Searcher

Oh Lord, my heart is filled with pain; I search for him in everyone I know. I'm realizing they don't have what I need. With tears rolling down my face, I cry, HELP, HELP, HELP ME Lord, I am dying in this mess. I am desperate to know him. Oh, Lord, why is he hiding from me? I need to know Lord, it hurts, please restore me. I'm getting tired in this search. I looked everywhere, and I can't find him. It's as if he doesn't exist. I gave myself away to so many things, trying to find him. And now he is gone forever. Now I just have the memory of the pain and rejection. Oh Lord, please reveal to me the love I need. Through searching in people places and things, I now know what I was searching for was you. Lord receive me as the search ends.

~Queen AB

Letter 3: She really does Care

Never judge your parents by who you think they are without getting the facts
of the environment of parenting.
-Angela N. Brand

Dear Troubled Young Lady

Hey Angie, all your younger years you thought your mother really didn't care about you, or loved you like she should. You were angry at her because you felt it was her fault allowing your dad to keep you a secret. Because you are young and don't know what a mother thinks yet, you blame her, not knowing her struggle. Not knowing what she has been through; and not knowing the situation. Remember she was a child, having a baby by an older man.

You are hurt and angry because you want your father in your life and you don't understand why he rejected you. Let me share some wisdom with you, there comes a time in your life, when you will have to accept you will never have a relationship with your dad, so you look to your Heavenly Father, to be that dad you never had.

You knew she loved you and was concerned about you, but you never knew the love she had for you ran deeper than any other love you have ever felt on earth. A mother's love is unconditional, uncommon and unscripted. You thought about how she raised you, and what you saw was the evidence of her love for you. Okay, your childhood was sheltered to some extent, but you still saw and were exposed to too much.

Sometimes, as parents, we expose our children to things too early, neglecting the fact that the devil has a plan for their lives that will affect their children, sometimes for the rest of their lives. At the same token, the family you have, and what they did to you, helped to shape who you are today.

As you grow in forgiving your mother and you finally tell her the things you experienced as a child and how you really feel, your relationship will grow stronger and stronger as the years go by. You now have three children of your own and have made many mistakes in raising them. You will understand the hard decisions parents make to protect and provide for the children. You begin to realize, she only did and raise you according to the knowledge she had at that time. So relax and allow her love for you to heal you.

Prayer from a Troubled Lady

Lord, I want to thank you for the wisdom, of allowing me to see that my mother really cared about me. It took me having my own children to realize that our parenting skill comes from what we know, or what we have experienced. I take back every feeling of unforgiveness I felt at the time, every feeling of abandonment, or every bad thought that I may have felt about my mother. I now know that she did the best she could, with what she knew; nothing more, nothing less, and for that I will be forever grateful to her, for loving me the way she did. From the depths of my soul, I can truly say,

I love her'

Diary 1
Letter 4: Who Am I?

Discovering one's self is facing the hard-core reality of their situation
realizing that's not what defines them
-Angela N. Brand

Dear Identity Crisis

Life begins to turn, and now you are asking these questions, "Who Am I and what is my identity?" What happened to that little girl who had hopes of being someone special? What happened to that man, who is supposed to love you and make you his wife? What happened to you going to college to play basketball, and being a social worker? What happened to that preacher that would travel the world preaching the gospel of Jesus Christ? What happened to that pastor that would lead God's people? What happened to that apostle that as supposed to equip the leaders? What happened to that prophet that would speak a word of restoration to lost souls? What has happened to my identity; and Who Am I? Angela, you thought your identity was in titles, positions, people, places, and things, but baby girl, your identity are in God.

First, I want to start off by saying, how sorry I am, for what I put you through, you have been to hell and back, up the block, around the corner, to the sky and the moon looking for your identity, because I had no clue who you were. You battled with the question "Who Am I" for so many years, not knowing the hard-core truth of your identify. You suffered rejection, not accepting your life and everything that came with it.

Angela, I am so sorry I treated you wrong, and misplaced your identity. I am so sorry for misusing your body, giving it to men who didn't deserve it. I am so sorry for the guilt you carried being a single mother not really knowing who your daughter's father was and struggled to raise your kids on welfare for twenty years. You put your kids through a lot, living with no heat, no water, no lights and no food at times. Because of the identity crisis, your kids suffered, you felt guilty having three kids by three different men and none of them were the father they were supposed to be. So you raised them on your own, not knowing what motherhood was all about.

I am so sorry for abusing food for comfort, not taking care of your body as I should. Angie, I am so sorry for allowing people to treat you any kind of way, because I wanted to please them, putting your needs and emotions on the back burner as if they didn't matter; because I want people to accept and love me. Later I will discover that every balloon will burst from the pressure of holding things in, which will cause you to suffer from anxiety. You will explode and lash out with hurt and pain, striving to get freedom and peace. But that's ok, I learned to work through it and take care of your needs, wants, and desires. I learned to love you and make you feel special.

I am so sorry for the repeated heart breaks from the many relationships. You gave your heart, soul and spirit, trying to get love from men, when all you needed to do is love yourself first. I am so sorry

Angela with tears rolling down my face, for not being the woman you needed and wanted me to be. I learned to be the best you possible, you will eventually get to the point where we will discover your identity and become Fearless and Unstoppable. Let me tell you who you really are, as Lisa Nichols says, "It's not despite your past, but it's because of your past, that you are a woman with great Wisdom, Courage and Boldness."

You are what they call high class, and some say "bougie" but that's okay, own it and walk in it. You are a threat to the enemy and you cannot be stopped, because you are planted in good soil. You are an asset to the Kingdom of God; your gifts and talents will be used to set millions of people free from what you struggled with. You will also become the go to person for others to discover their identity and empower them to be become better versions of themselves. You are God's favorite child, and nothing can change that. You are a faithful and committed woman that has greatness to offer the world, you are a great mother, daughter and wife, to a man that will love, honor, cherish and yes, be faithful to you.

You will also become the curse breaker in your family, building a multi-million-dollar brand; you are a woman with a past that has used it to empower people all over the globe. On your journey in discovering who you are, you learned to *Take Ownership*: Take *Ownership of Who You Are, Where You Are, Where You have Been, and most of all, Where You are Going.* That became your company's motto and the principal of life you stand on; where you developed coaching programs around it. You learned that you were a product of your environment and your action in the past, was not who you are, it was the hurt and pain coming out of you.

Through that process you learned that where you are in life was just a result of where you been, the things you been involved in, and the people you have allowed into your personal space. The most important thing was "Taking Ownership" of your greatness, knowing who you are and whose you are.

Psalm of an Identity Crisis

Lord, I can hardly speak; I can't see anything I'm fumbling in the dark trying to find my way. I'm falling and can't seem to get up, and stand strong on my own. Lord, you said if I call upon you, you would come and save me. Lord, I'm in pain and agony trying to discover who I am, I searched everywhere and found nothing. I searched in people and they all failed me. I searched in bottles in the night, but still nothing. It wasn't until I searched within and found true joy and peace that overtook me like the night. Lord thank you for being I AM.

Letter 5: Your Mess became your Message:
A Letter from your Future

Never allow your past to define you, it was only a tool God uses to produce
GREATNESS and turn your Mess into your Message!
-Angela N. Brand

Dear Past

Hello past, this is your future; I'm writing you to let you know everything will be all right, and your future is bright. Wipe your tears, straighten your posture and hold your head up high. See, in the past, you have fooled everyone else, but you did not fool me; I know what you really thought. I know what you have done and tried to hide it from everyone else. I know you, I was there, and I saw what they did. I remembered the tears and the fears, I remembered being in strange places, doing strange things with people who did not see your value. I am you, and I know your intimate thoughts. See, everything you are going through, God has a plan to use it for his glory.

The devil tried to abort your destiny, but God's power over ruled him. I'm writing this letter to you from a whole place. I see you were broken, wondering why me? Why did I have to go through all this? I felt your pain, I still feel it, and the pain of other women, hearing their stories of brokenness and losing the passion to live because the torment ran so deep within them. During my journey to getting back to you, I have talked to many young girls that have been where you are right now. But they weren't ready to let go and forgive the people that wronged them and live the life of freedom. Princess you found joy in your tribulations. You found love in your distress; you found peace in your storm.

God saw your heart and heard your secret prayers, seen your tears and heard you crying yourself to sleep at night, waking up with your eyes bloodshot red, sore and swollen, barely able to open them. He told me to tell you to let go of the pain, focus on your inner healing and forgive your father and the six men who molested and raped you, all the men that lied, cheated, and took advantage of you, including your ex-husband; but mostly, forgive yourself from the guilt, shame, and the embarrassment. You have been carrying the weight of it all by yourself, and now it's time for the Queendom Release.

I Release you now from all of it; I Release you to live and live more abundantly. I Release you to prosper and be in good health. I Release you to love and be loved. I Release you into your Destiny and Purpose. I Release you to be healed and to be Free. I Release you to give your Mess to the world, as your Message, no more shame, no more guilt, and no more regret. Angela, you are a beautiful mess with a message. Now be free, be made whole, and most of all, baby, Be YOU! Shine so Bright that you light up the world.

Psalms of a Queen

Lord, I thank you for bringing me out of everything I have been through. I thank you for covering me when I didn't want to be covered. I thank you for allowing your spirit to rest on the inside of me. Lord, thank you from the bottom of my heart and the depths of my soul, and for your mercy and grace, when I stepped out your will. I am humbled by your presence that you continue to allow me to feel it even when my flesh took over me. You didn't give up on me. You didn't turn your back on me. Instead, you showed me your love and kindness. I thank you, because through my mess, you gave me wisdom, knowledge and understanding, of who I was and my true assignment, and now you use me all over the world, to proclaim your message, and set the captives free.

Diary 2
The Birthing of a Queen
Co-Author Turkessia J. Barnes

Letter 1: Forgive Me, Forgive Me Not!

The art of forgiving is releasing one's self from making mistakes,
knowing they are growing tools.
-Angela N. Brand

Dear Queen,

can't do it! I just can't let it go, you thought to yourself; you wanted to walk forward, but your knees buckled, your heart sunk in despair and your mind keeps telling you it's your fault. The world says it's a result of the decisions you made, but you felt that this only partly true. You just wanted someone to love you; at least that's what you thought. You didn't know that the "V" in Love meant Virtue, and not the opening of your legs.

You are sick at the thought of taking a life, on two separate occasions; how you could have done such a thing, again, you thought. You lie awake at night, just the thought of it cause you to experience agony. It felt like there was no meaning to life, so the spirit of suicide followed you and tried to bury you, literally.

Forgiving others seem easier and easier by the moment, you can think of many people you can forgive right now, even the ones you thought played a part in these separate destructions, and all you have left, is the guilt that hovers over you like a black cloud. Nothing seems to hunt you more than you; you have become the spirit that once followed you, *her* name is depression. You are feeling low and unwanted; you are lashing out at everyone. Their spirit reminded you of familiar places and relationships that never lasted; you don't know who to call on or who to talk to, because nothing ever lasts.

You remember lying on that table asking God to forgive you for the premeditated decision, you made. The guidance counselor of the facility said that you had a choice, but this was your second time at the clinic in a single week, trying to get anyone to see and understand. You wanted this baby in your heart, but at 19, with no real sense of life, you could not take care of a new life. Besides, your family was waiting for you to arrive home, without a child. You sure didn't want to disappoint, "so was it was really your choice, right?" you asked yourself.

The doctor began to inject the medicines; it made every part of you numb, even your heart. As the medicines began to run through your body, and the tears fell from my eyes, the doctor said, "Good Morning, Ms. Barnes, here is the last ultrasound of your baby," in the quickness of the flash of the monitor, you saw your baby asleep, as if God had already given it peace. Your eyes began to close, and by the time you woke up, it was all over.

Years passed, and the pathway to forgive yourself became harder and harder to do. One day, you asked, will *not* forgiving yourself keep you out of heaven, will it keep you in bondage? Then, you asked God, if he had forgiven you? His answer was a resounding, YES. He said he had shown you forgiveness when he had blessed you with other children, he allowed you to keep.

In that moment, you were free, you no longer felt alone, later, you listened to an abortion help video to continue in your wholeness, it stated that you should name the children you aborted, on a piece of paper or an index card and pray over it. You did that, without hesitation, you prayed over it and released everything that day.

In that moment, you really believed that God could really love you, and you still do to this day. You stopped playing the mind games of *Forgive Me; Forgive Me Not*, because you know wholeheartedly, that nothing can ever separate you from the love of God. I want you to know the same, if you have ever found yourself playing the mind games of Forgive Me, Forgive Me Not" know that God wants you healed and restored. You can start your restoration with this simple prayer.

Prayer of a Queen

Lord, I come boldly to you, with a grateful heart, that you have allowed me to continue to live, even when I have taken a life, I thank you that you didn't let me die in the mess I created. Lord, I thank you that you have healed my brokenness, I thank you that you have forgiven me and made me whole. I thank you that I am no longer heavy or bound, but I can sleep, I can think more clearly and have a new outlook on life, knowing that your love, has saved and rescued me from all known and unknown things.

But, most of all of Lord, I thank you for saving me from myself. I am better because of you. I ask you God to please save me and the children I aborted, and to please give us rest. Lord, I thank you for not looking down upon me with disgust, but loving me despite of me, and my choices.

Lord, today I am asking you to rid me of the shame and guilt; but help me to be able to share my story so that other woman like me will know they can keep their children, they can love them, and that every assistance needed is already available.

I thank you Lord, that I will no longer walk with my head bowed down, but held high, knowing that you are the lifter of my head. I even thank you Lord, for every party involved in my mess, that you bring them great peace, knowing they gave their best advice during this time.

asked that you heal us all, so Lord, today I give you full access to my life, to come into my heart and guide me from this day forward, so I can be the Queen, you created me to be.

Sincerely, Forgiven

Letter 2: Congratulations, you made it, Girl!

You are your biggest cheerleader: congratulate yourself even when
all odds are against you.
-Angela N. Brand

Dear Queen,

Congratulations, you made it girl! You defeated what seemed impossible. Statistics states that you should have only completed half a semester at college, but congratulations, you made it girl! You went on to complete papers beyond your English level of comprehension, but congratulations, you made it girl!

You remember that day you got drenched in the rain, you would turn around and go back home, but congratulations, you made it girl! Even after that guy, who said he loved you, got you pregnant and disappeared...Ha! Congratulations, you made it girl! Those long nights in the library because the internet was off at the house, congratulations, you made it girl!

Remember that day your computer crashed with your 20+ page paper that was due the next day? Congratulation, you made it girl! Walking in the dark to the bus stop scared, with your mace in hand, with God following close behind, congratulations, you made it girl!

They said, *Honey,* if you didn't get it by now, maybe you should give up, but Congratulations, you made it girl! Remember, the day your grandmother passed after Reading class, you thought life had come to an end, but congratulations, you made it girl!

The first time you flunked your Algebra Class was a breakdown like no other, but congratulations, you made it girl! Remember being pregnant with London, and staying out two semesters, everyone thought it was over, but you pulled through and after one semester you were back in online classes and rocking it, congratulations, you made it girl!

The sacred days not knowing if you would make it, but congratulations, you made it girl! Had a few drop outs and even some that died, but Congratulations, you made it girl! Remember that Apartment Industry Management Training that guaranteed you that job you never received, but congratulations, you made it girl! Working long hours with 11:59pm deadlines, but congratulations, you made it girl!

Looking back, you began to see that it was only God's hand on your life that really got you to this place of victory. You didn't have a long list of great scholars that helped you to a bigger picture. You had to become the example. Now, you can pave the way for your children's children to see that education does mean something.

Every moment carried its own sense of grief when you think you're not going to make it out on top. It's kind of impossible to hold back the tears, but I wanted you to know that everything still worked out. You completed two degrees in Business Management and Human Resource Management, you made Deans' List and received a host of certifications, and you even gave birth, to two baby girls at that.

You were tested, you made mistakes, you kept pressing, you kept growing, you kept learning, you were the first of your mother's children to graduate from college and in the process; you were the epitome of someone who never gave up. You were taught wisdom in situations you never knew existed. You learned how to receive from complete strangers, and how to love from a distance. You learned how to be a team player, and at the same time, learned how to stand alone. I am most proud of you because you never gave up on you.

Dropout rates continue to decrease, because many have learned that education can have a bigger impact on their lives than ever before, many Queens are going back to school, after raising their children, and grandchildren, it's encouraging to see, and it gives you a sense pride, when you were told it could not be done, but, you got it done anyways.

You, decided to go to school with your children, it afforded you some moments in which you thought your only choice was to give up, but you pressed and made it through.

So, *Congratulations Girl, YOU Made IT!*

Prayer of a Self-Supporter

Jesus, you did it for me time and time again, and I will never forget the countless times you completely blew my mind, the instant connection, that linked me from level to level and even the times you wrapped your arms around me.

Today, I pray you help every Queen, trying to make a difference in their families lives, continue to wrap your loving arms around them all.

Sincerely,
Your Biggest Supporter!

Letter 3: The Joys of Motherhood

Motherhood is not a burden; it's a gift from God to bring life in this world.
-Angela N. Brand

Dear Queen,

Your heart was the heaviest it will ever be, in the corner of your bedroom, you sat in the same spot for a week, staring at the wall, sometimes screaming, but mostly crying, angry and way past depressed It was such a dark place, this spirit you had experienced much earlier was now creeping up, and its darkness had taken over your mind and taken over you.

This time you had to find the strength to fight, you couldn't just take a shower and wash it away, as you often did as a child, this time was different, and it had more rage, more pain and more hurt. You didn't want to do anything; everything seemed like way too much.

"How did you get to this place?" you wondered. You began to replay all the areas of your life that made you most shameful, most resentful and just plain bitter. You realized you were a complete mess; a rollercoaster of emotions, loud screams from your newborn baby was a cause for frustration, every scream brought about a new level of irritation.

You were gone, the more you sat in this place, the heavier it began to feel. You had no energy for anything; simple tasks like brushing my teeth and bathing were no longer at the top of your list. Flashbacks of past rejection from everywhere and everyone came rushing, one memory after the next, you couldn't stop it; it was like a big screen of your life playing over and over.

You had unexplained crying spells, holding it in never solves any problem and you never learned how to release your emotions because most times, you felt that nobody really cared. You remembered when you hadn't eaten in days, and your two-year old was getting food for herself, you felt worthless, inferior and just plain pathetic.

You must have been out of your mind because you can't even sit near a wall too long without feeling claustrophobic. It most definitely would have given you a headache or a real case of motion sickness. It wasn't until after your newborn had cried herself to sleep that you began to hear a faint whisper of words coming from your daughter's room, it was London, as you sat quietly and still.

You began to hear her praying for you, she was literally asking God for food, asking God to help you in the best way she knew how. My daughter had eaten every prepared snack, drank every juice and had given her sister every bottle there was. Sadly, that wouldn't be the last day you needed her prayers, but that day was your last day in that corner. You began to think, you have someone to fight for, and the truth was they've been there with you all along. You learned that you can't always look for comfort in the same place you give it, but you can locate it when it's really needed.

You know the women on television made it look effortless, just a few burps, a cute little cupcake smash to the face with a few crumbles and a Clorox wet wipe for easy cleaning. I mean, anyone could do it, or so you thought.

Motherhood seemed to be packed with joy, and lots of laughs. For some people, that may very well be the case, as for you, it was full of great joy and great pain all at the same time. Staring at your younger self, you thought, boy, do I have a lot to say; but what you can truly say, is that everything worked out just as planned. You now cherish each day and although sometimes, you feel like you are still not fit, you keep fighting to do better each day you are alive. Oh, The Joys of Motherhood, God sure saw fit to choose you.

Prayers of a Mother

Lord, today I am asking you to watch over and protect every mother. Lord, let them know that they are not alone. Let them know, that you are covering and shielding them, bless them and their seeds so that they can in turn bless others. God, create an unbreakable bond with your love, as you did for me, show them Lord, that you can bring us to a place of complete victory as we hold on to your words and never let go.

Lord, do not let them give up on themselves or you continue to send men and woman their way, to bless and love them with a righteous love. I thank you in advance for bringing every mother to the realization that they are enough, and through you all things are completely possible.

Please wrap them in your loving arms and hold back the forces of the enemy that try to destroy them; and pull them out of every dark place and every dark thought, for you are the light they need. Thank you for being the sunshine in the rain, and the light that will bring them out of what feels like a tunnel, even when they feel stuck. Give them tunnel vision until they fully accept you as the light. In Jesus name, Amen.
Sincerely,
A Whole Mother!

Letter 4: You are Enough!

Understanding you were born with everything you needed inside you to complete
whatever task God has given you
-Angela N. Brand

Dear Enough,

I think you are unaware of just how much power you possess. You are unaware of the understanding of what you have, and the genuine love you carry. There's a lot to say about a girl like you, that never gives up on herself, and while everyone is saying you can't, you always shock them with an, *I can, and I will* kind of attitude.

I think you are unaware that you are such a success because real success is what you make it, not what others say you should have. I think you are unaware that you are gifted in many ways, with every gift there's a special spirit of excellence that follows everything you do. I think you are unaware that you are the apple of God's eyes, and honey! Only His eyes will matter until the end of time.

I think you are unaware that you have such amazing potential, and that anything you put your hands to will prosper. I think you are unaware of just how anointed you are, so much so that God won't stop using you until his perfect work is done. I think you are unaware of the strong-minded person you have become; because you have beaten what tried to beat you.

I think you are unaware that love will come, because it will start with you. I think you are unaware that you are amazing, and it burst out in everything you do. I think you are unaware that you are worth it because you just simply are. I think you are unaware that you are favored because everything you set your mind to achieve is granted. I think you are unaware of just how smart you are because you think you are not. I think you are unaware just how bold you are because people try to make you feel timid.

Everything about you is bringing life and meaning to it, and it is demonstrated in your confidence. You have an abundance of light that shines brightly through you. I think you are unaware of just how creative you are, and what your mind can bring to life, whatever it's presented with. You are so optimistic, even the deadest of situations can be brought back to life. I think you are unaware of the joy you bring, because no one can meet you without smiling. My only wish is that you would be way less harmful to your mind and speak more positively to yourself. I want you to stop struggling with the thought that you deserve less. I want you to know you'll be the first to achieve so much in your family, so keep going, you are building a legacy.

I want you to know that every step you take, you are going in the right direction. I want to take this moment to reassure you about something I know you are painfully unaware of right now; Girl, you are enough! In life, we must come to the realization that "*You are Enough*", it comes from continuous prayer and a steadfast mindset. If you are constantly focused on who you are, and what you are not, you will then find fulfillment in the small things.

Prayer of Enough

Lord, we thank you that we view ourselves just as you view us. Help us realize that we are the apple of your eyes, we are the head and not the tail, above and never beneath, and we are the lenders and not the borrowers, and that no matter how hard it is to see sometimes, we will still always believe that God sees us as enough.

Thank you for carrying us when we are down, helping us keep our faith and move past the hurdles that sometimes weigh our heart down. Help us to know that we are enough, just the way you created us to be, and because of your unconditional love, we thank and praise your name for it all.

In Jesus name, Amen.

Sincerely,

I AM Enough!

Letter 5: Searching Within

Searching within is the art of mastering one's self true talents and abilities to discover their identity.
-Angela N. Brand

Dear Searcher,

It would take you years to find but you were still going to search. It would take you years to reach, but you were still going to search. It would take you months later to get a grip, but you were still holding on. It would take you to places where your breath would almost fail, and yet you would be still alive to tell.

It would take you through moments of guilt and even more shame. You can still remember the soft whispers saying "Girl, you can do this!" You would even go on to have two more pregnancies before you finally said, enough is enough. As a woman, you know what's good for you, even before you really know. You just wish you would have trusted your instincts, trusted yourself.

But, it would take you more lies and empty promises; it would take you more tears and sleepless nights, for the truth to be revealed. There was always something about life that lets you know when there's something wrong, but there's something about your process that brings it to its rightful end. It felt like a book that wouldn't end; you thought, "well at least he's not hitting me," but sometimes his words did all the punching necessary. It felt like an aisle full of damaged goods; thinking who would want you, want us, because you have two children now.

It would take you years to find what you are looking for, but you were still going to search. It would take another canceled date, but you would still find time to reschedule. It would take me another cancelled engagement, but you still held on.

It would take you months to know you were enough and, discover God in a new way before you would completely forgive. It was then that you realized, you were searching for the love that always lived within you, not in a man, not in any relationship; it would only take you a second before you realized, and that God's love is what kept you.

So today I pray for you:

Prayer of a Searcher

Dear God,

We thank you for this great new opportunity to make things right. We also thank you for always being the love we needed, we come before you humbly, and we worship you for being God.

Before we ask you for anything else, we ask that you forgive us for anything we have done or said that was not pleasing in your sight. We thank you for making our minds strong and our hearts more available to you. God, you are everything to us, and we need you like never before, to shower us with your great love, grace and favor.

We understand that our testimonies will be used by you and we thank you for every valley low and every high place. We thank you for the good and even the bad. Give us great peace in knowing that everything is working for our good.

You are our great comforter and our great God in whom we trust. Help us to please you, love ourselves as you have instructed us to do. Give us the grace to thirst after you for wisdom, and to look for it in our everyday life.

We desire to find great wisdom in every conversation, and everything we encounter. We want to be courageous, and to desire growth for our soul, and relationship with you.

In Jesus name, Amen.

Diary 3
#Self-Love the Journey
Co-Author Courtney Smith

Letter 1: Insecurities on a Silver Platter

You were never served doubt, fear, or rejection. When God serves you something, you can always find security.
-Angela N. Brand

Dear Insecure

Here you are at the sweet age of 16 living your life and trying to fit in while feeling blocked out. I know it was hard trying to find your way and understand who you are authentically. School was very hard for you; oftentimes you would find yourself comparing yourself to others. You always wanted to be that girl who had the pretty hair, small waist, that cute shape and that outgoing personality that got her the attention that you felt would validate you as a young teenager.

Do you remember going home and locking yourself in your room trying on different clothing seeking to feel accepted, and looking through magazines trying to take on an image that was not yours? Do you recall the times you would write letters to yourself wishing and praying to God that he would make you smaller and beautiful and give you a personality that would stand out, so you would feel wanted, needed and desired? Or better yet, do you remember those moments you would decline invitations to hang out with your friends, simply because you knew they were going to be around so many other people and you literally would get social anxiety? You were constantly telling yourself that you are not pretty and talented or good enough for any boy to like you or see you at the top of the pick. Instead of blossoming and standing out, you found safety in being shy, quiet, and mediocre and reserve. You allowed your insecurities to take away some of the best years of your life; it did not have to be that way, but because you refuse to believe in who you are and whose you are, you allowed your insecurities to reside in your mind and spirit, as if on a platter, and guess what, you ate every crumb, which is why those lies and insecurities became a part of your false identity.

Today at this very moment you are being reborn; you are getting a second chance to regurgitate and expel those lies of not being enough, smart enough or intelligent enough; or even loved, wanted, needed, valued and desired. This is the moment I give you permission to embrace you for what you truly are. No longer will those insecurities rule and reign over your life. Trust me when I tell you that no matter what others may think of you or what they may say, you are perfect even in your imperfections. When God stitched you in your mother's womb, he knew that you were going to be perfect, simply because you were created in his image. So, promise me that the next time you are served a silver platter, lift the lid and take a deeper look. If it's those same old insecurities from the past are there, let the enemy know your life has changed and from this point on, you are only eating the truth of what God says you are and nothing less.

Psalms of the Insecure

My Lord and Savior, my Way Maker, my Lilly of the valley, my Healer, my Redeemer and my Friend, thank you for loving me. So many years I have struggled with insecurities that seem to alter who I am and what I want to become. I am so glad I know your spirit and the power it possesses. You told me years ago how special and unique I was, but because I feed my mind with my personal thoughts and beliefs about me, I could not open my heart and allow your words and your truth to override what I have been pouring into my spirit for you so long.

Thank you for healing me, thank you for covering me, thank you for giving me enough wisdom to yield and lay before your throne, confessing to you my deep, horrific, depiction of what I believed about myself. Thinking that you would push me away and judge me, I was quite scared. Once I realized that you loved me no matter what, I was able to embrace Courtney and everything that came along with her. It was not easy, but with you Lord, you made it better. Now, if I must be honest, there are some things that I am still working on, so I can become the best version of myself and guess what it is "OK". I give you all the honor, glory, and praise because you love me I can now learn to love myself.

Amen
#SELFLOVE

Letter 2: Reflections of Her Inner Soul

True reflections are not measured from the outside or one's surroundings, it what's within that make the true soul.
-Angela N. Brand

Dear Inner Soul

You are truly living your life like its golden; here you are a 23-year-old woman who has her own, I am so proud of you. To be quite honest, I am surprised you beat the odds, let's see; you graduated high school with no kids, that summer you got accepted into college and not one moment did you ever thought about giving up or giving in to the pressures that life brought you. Instead, you decided to keep pushing.

As time went on you graduated from college, landed a great corporate job that allowed you to move out and start your life as Ms. Independent. However, you forgot to handle some things, you know the matters of your heart and your addiction to the comparison. Yeah, you were miss goody two shoes, miss church girl, miss do the right thing; but you had issues that you hid deep down in the pit of your infected soul. I must say, you hid them well, not even your best friend knew you had these demons that you invited in to take resident in your mind. What was wrong with you Courtney? It seems as if you took pleasure in tormenting yourself with these lies and thoughts that was the total opposite of WHO you truly are or at least what God says you are.

I understand you had an image to uphold, and so many people looked up to you for advice, but you neglected you in the process. Let's be real, you pretended to be miss perfect, but you HATED YOURSELF. The outer shell of who you were was a pecan tan, brown sugar complexion, nice smile, lovely dimples, shoulder length dark pretty hair, 5 ft 3, that was okay. I mean, I didn't have a body of a goddess, but it worked, clearly, you were a beautiful black woman. Now can I tell you the truth? None of that mattered, it didn't matter because on the inside you were broken, angry, bitter, jealous of the next woman, spiteful, vindictive; your soul was U.G.L.Y.

Years of feeling unworthy, the constant comparison of yourself to other "quality" women, the dishonorable meaningless relationships all played a part in who you really were. I wished you would have dealt with those demons instead of suppressing them. You were dying inside, and instead of addressing the issues, just to save face you masked it, living a lie. So, for years you hated yourself, and for years you were a dead woman walking, hiding behind the false illusions that you had your shit together. You didn't; you were a hypocrite. You did not find anything wrong with you ministering; giving advice, healing others, yet your soul was bleeding out into your spirit. Courtney, you were drowning in your own sorrows, yet you refused to help yourself.

Take a deep breath and dry your eyes. I know I sound a little harsh, but you must realize that you and you alone were holding the gun to your own head, pulling the trigger daily because you did not want to confront the reflection of your inner soul.

Praise be unto GOD, who will keep you from falling. I am so glad you surrender and asked God to have HIS way in your life. I am so glad you realized the heaviness of putting on a mask was killing your total being as a woman. Simply because you surrender, you are now set free from those lies of the enemy. You can now authentically practice what you preach, the infection has healed, the bleeding has stopped you have been delivered!

I am so proud of you Courtney; you do not always get this thing called life right but accepting who you are and trusting what God says about you has made you such a better person. Now go in peace, beloved, be blessed!

Psalms of an Inner Soul

Lord, I want to lie beside the green pasture and allow you to restore my soul; Like David, create in me a clean heart. As I gaze deeply, let my sight penetrate my soul, so I can examine myself and call forth those lies the enemy has tried to tell me about me. By your grace and mercy, Lord God, I ask that you pluck that infected vessel from its root, so it will not take over my precious life

For I know that for me to be true to who I am, and love me the total woman of God, I must always allow myself to be checked by your spirit, Lord. I am grateful that you were right there with me in my battles. I know that with seasons life will change, so when it does, endow me with wisdom, clarity and your word to pull down any stronghold that is designed to show me something different from what you have said to be true about me. No more, jealousy, comparison, bitterness, strife, or self-hate. Thank you for loving me, without your love I would not have been able to love me apologetically.

Amen

#SELFLOVE

Letter 3: Bed of Death

Never lay sleep in a place that was meant to bring you life!
-Angela N. Brand

Dear *Bed of Death*

I know you feel like life is beating you up right now; I know you feel like your prayers are falling on deaf ears. In the last three years, you had to bury your brother, pull the plug on your father and walk away from a marriage that was no longer a marriage. Your heart took a mighty blow back to back, without having any time to heal. Life did not care that you were a mother of three little ones, that you had a home to manage, that others were depending on you for everything, while trying to put together the pieces of your once, *happily ever after*. I know it was too much for you; not only was your heartbreaking, but your soul was shattered as well. To make matters worse, you had to deal with you for 24 hours a day, even after your friends left. The pain, the anxiety, fear, depression, and hopelessness rushed in like a tsunami!

Do you remember that voice that whispered and told you to end it all? Deep down inside you knew it was wrong, but what the *fuck*. How much pain can one woman take?! I know you didn't want to kill yourself, but at the time death in your sleep sound pleasant than having to deal with a broken heart, a shattered soul and all the *bullshit* life had to offer you. I totally get it, and not to mention GOD, you felt, was refusing to be your shelter in a time of a storm. Death was sweet, so why not? Here you are on the bed of death, pills in my right hand, and the alcohol in my left. I even recall you counting down the moment 3, 2, 1. WOW, you of all people, who would have thought, SUICIDE? At the time you didn't care, you just did not want to hurt anymore, and I get it, and I forgive you. I wish I was there then to tell you it wasn't going to work. You are not God; you do not have the right to take away the life He gave you. I wish I was there to speak to your spirit and awaken the God within, to tell you to stop fighting in your own strength but yield to him who can keep you from falling. I wish I was there to tell you this too shall pass, do not do it. Thank God for mercy, because that night as you planned to take your own life, God's grace and mercy said NO. I am so glad He did, now you are able to not only exist, but you get a chance to live. You get a chance to live a new life and take back your power to make the best out of the cards that life dealt you.

Psalms of a Queen

Wonderful and merciful God that you are, forgive me for not trusting you, forgive me for not moving out of the way and letting you handle those issues I thought I was strong enough to fix. I am grateful to know your spirit, grateful to feel your presence, and grateful to hear your voice. There are so many women who share my story. Jesus, I pray you breathe a fresh anointing over their mind, body, and spirit. Suicide, suicidal thoughts and attempts are the trick of the enemy. Tricking many into believing that taking their lives is easier than trusting you in the difficult moments that life will bring. I pray you cover these women; remove the scale from their eyes so they can always find you in the middle of their darkest moments. Hold them close to you Lord, rock them to sleep and give them peace that surpasses all understanding. Amen

#SELFLOVE

Letter 4: Pills, Pain to Purpose

Don't allow your pain to push you away from your purpose; your pain will produce purpose in its season.
-Angela N. Brand

Dear Pain

There you are, thirty years old with three kids and alone; wanting to escape a reality you felt compelled to be, what were you thinking? Clearly, you were not and guess what, your attempt to end it all failed, why, you ask? Because GOD had a plan for your life and he loved you so much that he wanted to answer that prayer you prayed a few days ago. Do you remember? Let me help you. "God, if you deliver me from this I promise you I will not let my heartbreak and setbacks be in vain, I surrender, have your way". So, that morning when you woke up and saw the sun bursting through your blinds, that was God speaking to your spirit, telling you to rise and live. Yes, it was difficult and extremely hard, but you did it. Daily you tried to put one foot in front of the other crying and feeling weak, lost, confused, angry, and depressed, but you did it. I am so proud of you.

I am grateful for your decision to lean and depend on God to pull you up out of your death bed, so that the prayer can be fulfilled. As time went on you began to work on you falling in love with you all over again. Yeah, I know all the other times you tried, but this time it was something different. This healing was the healing that you needed not just for yourself but for others.

See, Courtney you had to endure it, so GOD can reveal your calling and your purpose in life. You are who God says you are and nothing less. Continue to heal because your healing will heal others.

Prayer of a Queen

Lord, often in life we never know why things happen to us. Right now, it seems that you are so unfair, unloving and that you do not care about us. Many of us feel that if you loved us the way you say you do then why must we endure these deathly heartbreaks, setbacks, and disappointments. Then we realize that you are sovereign and that you have a way of working all things out for our good. For that alone God, I say thank you.

    Thank you for keeping me when I could not keep myself. Thank you for speaking to me that morning commanding me to rise and take my bed and walk. You gave me a new life and divine anointing that revealed to me who I was and who I shall be in you. I am so glad I know your spirit Lord, daily I ask you endow us with the power and endurance that we need to take up our cross and live authentically for you. Just like that light that burst through my window and revived my soul, let me be that same force of light to help heal, guide and coach others who may be laying in their own bed of death.

Amen
#SELFLOVE

Letter 5: When She gave God Her "YES"

Allow your Yes to give God permission to give His Yes to the promise
He has for you
-Angela N. Brand

Dear Yes

Come here Courtney and have a seat; now I know you are thinking that this shit is too hard, not fair, extremely complicated, and depressing as Hell. See, now that your divorce is final, you are moving on with your life and your plans to be a better you but there is something missing. The reason why you are frustrated and often find yourself on an emotional roller-coaster is because you have not totally surrendered your ALL to God.

This brokenness, this unhappiness, and this unbalanced life you are trying to carry and put together is an epic failure because you are refusing to move out of the way. I know at this point in your life you are discovering your calling, and I must say you are helping women heal from their broken places by sharing your story and telling your truth, and for that, I am proud of you.

You, my love, have come a long way from that deep dark hole of depression and worrying, which was the birthing ground for anxiety and that suicidal bed that almost claimed your life. No, the road was not easy, in fact, it was a battle, and by God's grace and love, He has shown you how to survive. However, the residue from your past still rears its ugly head at times, and instead of dealing with it, you tried to ignore it. I am so glad the feeling of torment became unbearable, that you learned how to seek God's face, get out the ring, stop fighting your battles, and simply give God your "YES".

Knees bent, and body bowed, you surrendered that day and gave Him all of you. With the resilience of a queen you realized that you did not hold the antidote to reassemble your broken heart and put back the pieces of your fragile spirit where it belongs. I can shout Hallelujah, thank you JESUS!! How you got over that storm. Now, at this very moment I call you healed, whole, complete, humble, and tenacious. I salute you, my queen, because of your walk and your journey of shifting your hurt to healing that I can exist. In this very moment, I am happy, free, and more than anything else, I have found my purpose in Christ Jesus, all because the old you gave God your YES.

Prayer of a Yes

Oh Lord, there is nothing more uncertain than living a life not knowing. Understanding that life is not scripted and that we have no clue what exactly tomorrow will bring. Dealing with life and all the pressures and uncertainties it will bring, teaches us Father how to find rest and comfort in you. For you said in your words Lord, if we keep our minds stayed on you, you will keep us in perfect peace. Lord, teach us how to depend on you; knowing your word is a solid foundation we can stand on without worrying about being let down, mistreated, neglected or abused.

Lord, we understand we are co-laborers with you, which means we must play our part, to do so Father, we must surrender our will and our way and give you our "yes." In exchange, we are able to hear from you what we are called to do. Father, let every woman who is hurt, alone, afraid, broken, mistreated, abused and neglected, feel your presence and your anointing, may it fall fresh upon her daily. For I was once that woman and because of you I am set free. As your child, I am standing in the gap for my sisters asking that you endow them with the courage to give you their "YES". Amen

#SELFLOVE

Diary 4
After the Storm
Co-Author Georgia Gayle

Letter 1: Stolen Innocence

What seemed like it was stolen, was restored by God
-Angela N. Brand

Dear Stolen Innocence,

I remembered how you felt: wondering why this monster's hands were forever in your underwear, wondering why it hurt when you peed, wondering why you were always tender in that region. Wondering why your private parts were never private, it's as if they belonged to someone else. You were wondering when rescue was going to come, who was going to save "Lisa," who was going to stand up for you, who was going to tell you that your innocence, that was being violated was not your fault; it was the actions of a sick and perverted human being.

I remember you thinking that you were a nobody, and damaged goods, no one would believe you anyway, your father was the village drunk who could not protect you; mama would think you were a bad girl who wanted this to happen and would give you a beating. I remembered the feeling of outrage you felt, even at eight, you knew something was wrong with what he was doing, it was not right; no matter what the monster said, something in you knew he was lying, or was he?

I remembered how you felt when the monster died, he thought he was invincible, but he found out the hard way that God protects his own and will never leave or forsake them. I remembered how happy you felt; the torture was finally over, how hopeful you felt, knowing you could grow up normal; now your monsters could stay in the books you were always reading, now they can be imagined, instead of real.

I am here to let you know, you mattered, you will go on to be violated, raped and hurt beyond measure, but you matter, everything will turn out okay. You will persevere, you will conquer, and you will have the battle scars to prove how strong you really are. The monster thought he could bury you, he forgot that you were a seed that needed time to germinate, and now you have become that beautiful flower you were always supposed to be, fully whole and delivered.

Psalm of an Innocence Stolen

n my distress I called on you, and you rescued me, you picked me up
n your loving arms and took the monster away from my life. He was
gone, just when he thought he could torment me forever. I just want to
say how grateful I am to you God for all you have ever done for me and
will continue to do for the rest of my life, you are my rock and my
fortress, and I will continue to trust you.

Letter 2: Scared and Pregnant

Regardless how afraid you are, just know God is always protecting you.
-Angela N. Brand

Dear, Scared and Pregnant

You were 18 and pregnant; I remembered how scared you were, how were you going to tell mama that her little girl who she thought was perfect, was not so perfect after all? How was daddy going to take the news? I remembered you thinking how stupid you were believing some boy's lies when he told you that could not get pregnant the first time; I remembered you thinking, how much longer could I hide the fact I was with child from my mama, this was not something that going away, this was something that was coming, no amount of ignoring and pretending was going to work this time.

You could still see the shock in mama's eyes when she looked at you that look of disappointment that flooded over her face when she finally realized that you were already seven months pregnant; all hell broke loose for a while. All you could do was cry and wondered what was next? Daddy was not home yet, what would happen when he came home and find out? Being scared did not begin to describe how you felt; it was like the world was coming to an end.

As expected, daddy kicked you out of the house the very next day, you had to stay with a friend for two months until she told you, you had to go back home to have your baby. I remembered one of your very best friends taking you in, and you stayed at her house until your baby was born. I remembered how chaotic it was, since mama left for the United States three days before your baby was born.

The day came when you had to go to the hospital because you went into labor, you went by yourself, no mother, no father, no one; you are feeling like you were having an outer body experience. You quickly had to learn how to take care of a child, since you had no immediate experience to fall back on.

When I looked at all you went through, I wanted to tell you that everything was going to be ok; that the child you had is now thirty years old, that she turned out to be a beautiful, smart, hardworking, well-spoken woman, just like you. She is everything you wished for in a child; all the struggles and the hurt you felt, would make you and her the strong independent women you both are today.

I look back at you today and can truly say, "You done good girl," from that scared eighteen-year-old girl to the fifty-year-old woman you have become, and you look to the heavens and whisper, "thank you God."

Psalm of a Queen

I can truly say, God you were my refuge and my strength, you have been with me my whole life; you stood by me when times got rough, you protected and shielded me from the physical pain of childbirth, and the emotional pain of abandonment that I felt. Looking back, I realized that you have always been there, even when I could not see you, you were in the background carrying me though all the storms in my life, I am truly grateful.

Letter 3: New Beginnings

Sometimes things must end, before you can embrace the new beginnings
-Angela N. Brand

Dear New Beginnings

I am staring at a picture of you, trying to remember what you were feeling or thinking at that time, it was the year you came to America, 1988 and you were 19. By then you had already had your first child the previous year and was trying to live down the shame that you felt; while at the same time trying to start fresh, in a new country with new possibilities-after all, you were told that America was the land of opportunities, where anyone can become someone.

I looked at your smile in that picture, and I know the conflicted emotions taking place inside your head, how sad, happy, hopeful, scared and torn you felt. Worrying about the child you left behind in Jamaica, wandering if she was being taken care of the way you would have done it. I remembered the nights you went to bed crying your eyes out, longing for your child, feeling empty and alone, and not knowing it would take five long years to get her back.

I feel the need to let you know, that everything is going to be okay, that you just needed to trust God, that it was going to get rough for a while, but that you would be fine, don't worry so much, "this too shall pass," is what I would say to you, you are going to make some mistakes in love and in life, but someone, once said, "it is better to have loved and loss, than never to have loved at all." You are a people pleaser right now, caring more about what others think of you; being in a new country and trying to get everyone to like you. Understand, there are people who will take your kindness or your niceness for weakness and use it to their advantage.

Try not to think too much about things you can't control, forgive others, even though I know that's hard to do, be confident in the woman you are becoming, I know how difficult it is, but you can do this girl, you got this. I just wanted to let you know I am proud of the woman you are becoming, keep it up; you are doing a great job. By the way, you are a good mom to your child, not a perfect mom, but a good one none-the-less; you gave up your hopes, desires and dreams to make sure she had everything she needed. You did not have much, but you did the best you could, and that is all anyone can ask for.

I think back at you at nineteen and at look at you now fifty, and I am once again at the threshold of life's possibilities, and I find my past self, Lisa, and my current self, Geor-g-i-a, rushing towards a collision course with our destiny, at peace with everything that has transpired over the last fifty years, not living with any regrets, living a life that we always wanted and deserved, because after all, we are the child of a king, and that my dear, makes us royalty.

Psalms of a Queen

Thank you, God, for always being by my side, even when I came to this country, I left my heart in Jamaica; I cried for years missing my child, you comforted me though-out the journey; when I felt lonely or sad, you gave me your joy and peace, you are an awesome God, and without you I would be nothing.

Letter 4: Beaten

Regardless of the beating and attacks, God will always protect you and deliver you out of them all.
-Angela N. Brand

Dear Beaten,

I can still see the confused look on your face, as he slapped you so hard you fell on the other side of the bed, you were confused because he is telling you he loved you out of one side of his mouth, yet he is beating you at the same time. I can still see how scared you were, this man was supposed to be teaching you how to drive a Stick Shift, instead you ended with not one, but two black eyes.

I remembered how fearful you felt when he threatened to drive off the road in a cliff and end it all; or how you felt when you tried to break it off with him, but he would still followed you around, how he showed up at your job, at your house, your church, even after you had called the police and sign an order of protection against him. I remembered the last straw was when he showed up in your Math class at the college; how you left the class the moment he walked in and sat two seats behind you; how you ran to the registration office and dropped the class

I looked back and can now tell you why it happened; damage people attract other damage people, it's called the law of attraction, you attract who you are or who you think you deserved. I think about how broken this man was, growing up in foster care, his mother had 15 kids and did not raise any of them, and they bounce around in the foster care system until they become adults.

Despite everything you have been through, I wanted to let you know how strong I think you really were, how proud of you I am, you have been terrified at different junctions in your life, but you still made it out like a trooper, to become the strong independent woman you are today, I have you to thank for that.

Psalm of the Beaten

I cried out to the Lord, I asked him, "Where are you, why aren't you saving me?"And He heard and delivered me from this man who wanted to destroy me. He became my guide and my protector, my shield and butler. He made me see the fighter that was within me and gave me the strength to get away my abuser.

Letter 5: Born too Soon

Although we have dates and schedules, just know nothing happens
by mistakes
-Angela N. Brand

Dear Mother to Be,

It was the best and the worst day of your life all at the same time; I remembered how scared you were when you realized that the amniotic sac that held your second child, had ruptured when you were only six months pregnant. You thought about the fact that you had not seek your doctor's advice before leaving the States but had simply purchase a ticket and went to Jamaica. The guilt you felt; what if your actions had placed your child in danger, or maybe even worse.

The decision was made to head for the airport; you were numb with fear and worry. You sat on that plane, trying to keep as still as possible, trying not let on your high-risk pregnancy had gone from bad to worse. I remembered that the plan was to keep your condition under wraps until you were sure that you were no longer in the Islands but was back in the Americas, since you were not in pain, it was relatively easy, except for the fact that the fluid that kept the baby safe had not stopped trickling down, that was the only indication that anything was wrong.

If being scared was not already on the table, I remembered how it got much worse when you landed at JFK airport, and you were surrounded by immigration officers, suspicious of what was going on, or what your intentions were. You were repeatedly asked the same questions; all you wanted to do was to get to a hospital to be checked out, before continuing to the neighboring state of Connecticut where you lived.

I just wanted to let you know that it all turned out well, your baby was born 10 days later, she only weighed 3 pounds 7 ounces, you were told that she may have developmental learning issues and may be delayed, that turned out to be false, she grew into a beautiful, intelligent, young lady, getting ready to be 22 years of age.

Beloved, you have endured the storms, your innocence was violated by a monster, you got pregnant at an early age, you have been beaten, mistreated, you had to leave your first born child in Jamaica for five years, you endured having a premature baby, and having to leave her with strangers in a hospital for thirty days. I know you have been through a lot, yet you survived every attack like a *BOSS*. You are a survivor, and despite of it all, you have made it through. I just wanted to tell you how proud I am of you, you have accomplished a lot, you were the first in your immediate family to graduate from college, and become a bestselling author, and you have not even begun to scratch the surface.

You felt that because you came from the back bush of Jamaica, people like you do not become motivational speakers and life Coaches, yet with God's help you did that too. Every time someone says what we can and can't do, your response should be, 'WATCH ME."

Prayer of Thanksgiving

Thank you, God, for how you have had my back from the very beginning, you protected and kept me and my child safe throughout everything that we went through, you gave me the strength to stand on my own two feet when I did not think I could, thank you for all your many blessings you have given unto me.

Amen

Diary 5
The Woman Inside
Co-Author Mary J. Wade

Diary 5
Letter 1: Seize the Moment

Learn to live in the moment so you can embrace the right now, rather looking ahead and missing the lessons that will set your path straight
-Angela N. Brand

Dear Moment

We have all heard the saying, time flies, it is true, and it waits for no one. Each moment is all you have, seasons change, and life goes on. I just wanted to tell you to enjoy the journey along the way. Stop and smell the roses, hear the birds sing. Many live their entire lives without noticing the "moment". As a result, they miss the joy of life, only to realize that time has passed them by. Don't be that person. View each day as a present, a gift. Wake up with great expectation! Don't hold on to anger, and unforgiveness. This will take discipline, love and self-control. Love and self-control are the bookends of the fruits of the spirit. Without the same, you will lose time, and experience less than perfect health and happiness. You want to keep the fruits of the spirit at the forefront of your mind; Love, Joy, Peace, Kindness, Goodness, Faithfulness, Gentleness and Self-control.

Get rid of worry, it is a trap; it breeds fear, anxiety and mental illness. Worry robs you of your joy and is a waste of time. In fact, the bible commands us to "worry about nothing" and instructs us to pray about everything. Phil 4:6-7; do not be anxious (worry) about anything, but in everything, with prayer and supplication with thanksgiving, let your requests be made known to your creator. This requires a lifetime of self-checks. Worry takes you away from the "moment" and forces you in a place of anxiety, and the cycle continues.

Girl, worrying will kill you....there are more people in mental institutions and in the grave, than anywhere else because they worry themselves to death. Remember to speak life, your words have power! The power of life and death are in the tongue. Every word spoken into the atmosphere is made manifest, and every idle word will be judged. Be sure to speak over yourself in encouragement and dismiss every negative thought. Resist the enemy and he will flee, start your day with positive affirmations; this is the day that the Lord has made, you will rejoice and be glad in it. Everything you set your hands to do will prosper. You walk in unmerited favor; everyone attached to you is blessed. You are the head and not the tail, above only, and never beneath, you are healed, all is well!

There will come a day when you will have to say goodbye to your parents, relatives and friends. Tell them that you love them often. You will ruin relationships with family, with your condescending words and actions. So many times, you have heard or read that someone's biggest regret is not telling someone they loved them, not knowing you would not see them again in this earthly realm.

Seize the moment, take that trip, create that bucket list, then Go, Do, See! Dance like no one else is looking. Write the vision; you have a gift of seeing the beauty in the things God has created. Share this with others so they may also see, understand what truly matters in the temporal life, and live your best life NOW.

Prayer of the Moment

Great and Almighty Heavenly Father, be glorified. I ask you to help me to "let go" and seize the moment. I long to just enjoy the journey without worry. I have spent so much time living in fear about what could happen, feeling anxious, and screaming inside and out. Calm me and keep me in your care. You said you would keep me in perfect peace if I kept my mind stayed on thee. As such, I will meditate on your word and dismiss negative thoughts that try to rob me of the moment. Remind me to go to the secret place under the shadow of your wings.

Amen

Letter 2: Girl Get Your Purse Right!
Become Financially Literate

Never carry a purse worth more than your net worth. It's not what's in the purse that makes the worth, rather who is carrying the purse.
-Angela N. Brand

Hey Girl!

Very early in life, in fact now, you must learn how money works and become the CEO of your finances. Many people manage all the other areas of their life, but often neglect learning about the resources needed to meet their basic living expenses (food, clothing, shelter). Your best example is your parents, they took care of all your needs and you never missed a meal. This is because they understood the value of family first. You did not see a greed for materialism, but a love of family and provision; take care of the money you earn. Learn how to invest early in life. Ensure that you have a 401K established, along with savings, and be a giver.

Money is not the root of all evil, but the "love" or idolatry of money is. Used properly, it is a tool that can create a legacy for your family. It should also be used to bless others-he who gives with a generous eye will be blessed. When misused it leads to a life of misery, according to the bible, Proverbs 22:7 KJV "the borrower is slave to the lender." You will never be free until you are "debt free". One of the best pieces of advice my mom gave me was to "save for a rainy day." Without reparation a rainy day becomes a storm! This is also known as emergency savings, and everything becomes an emergency when you have no savings.

Helping others is commanded in this journey, but you cannot be a blessing until you can help yourself financially. There are several methods taught to gain control of your money. Research, and remember to *save some, spend some and give some*. Live below your means, you do not need the latest and greatest car, home or gadget. Things come and go, along with fads, be sure to start and keep a budget. Keep record of every penny spent, know where every dollar goes, do not fall into the debt trap .Credit cards are helpful in emergencies and for building credit, but often have high interest and hidden fees. Once you enter this vicious cycle, it is very hard to become debt free. Debt can lead to bankruptcy; bankruptcy will only create more misery, as it will ruin your credit, making it much more difficult to obtain the things you "need". It takes 7–10 years before a bankruptcy is removed from your credit file. Student loans are the biggest source of debt for Americans. Do everything you can to avoid them at all costs. Look for employer sponsored programs to further your education. Above all, use wisdom in your finances, and pray for guidance.

Prayer from a young Girl

Father, you are great, and greatly to be praised; protect me from the desire and greed of material gain. Help me to understand giving and receiving according to your perfect will. Keep my mind and heart pure knowing that all things come of thee, and that you own everything even the cattle upon a thousand hills. I desire to help others learn how to manage their finances. I have had to start over from nothing, and I thank you for showing me the way.

I ask in the name of the Yeshua the Christ

Letter 3: Know your Worth

Your worth is more than possessions, but it's the value that you carry inside you.
-Angela N. Brand

Dear Worthy Young Lady

So many young ladies fail to understand their value and their worth. I would implore you to understand that you are beautiful inside and out. You will not realize how beautiful you are until later in life. You will be a late bloomer; this is a gift in disguise, because your focus will be on things that will prepare you for life. Even if no one tells you that you are special, to thine own self be true. You are different, unique, fearfully and wonderfully made; you are the apple of your creator's eye! You will have many young callers, and well-meaning young men who will tell you anything and everything you want to hear, to get your body. They will say "I love you" which typically means "I lust you" and the moment you give yourself away, they walk away. Do not give yourself away. Wait for the one your Heavenly Father has for you. Understand that love is a word used in many ways, good and bad, true and false, and is often in vain.

Who can find a virtuous woman? For her price is far above rubies. Virtuous means having or showing high moral standards. Oh, how many times we have heard this in church, and to be honest, had no idea what it meant. Become a study of a Proverbs woman, because in the end she is the one a good man looks for in a wife. Present yourself as a virtuous woman, and you will attract a righteous man.

Most little girls play with baby dolls and dream of the fancy wedding and the dashing man who carries her away in a horse drawn carriage. This mindset while harmless it seems can also blind you into thinking that the first man who tells you they love you is honest. Word to the wise—love yourself unconditionally. Know what you have is a treasure that man cannot live without, which is worth more than gold. Even if you believe you are in love, know your worth.

Love yourself enough to let go of anyone who does not respect you, nor loves you and show it by his actions. Trust your creator for guidance to a full future of love with someone who cannot get enough of taking care of your heart. Believe it and receive it, for you know the plans God have for you, plans to prosper you and not harm you, and plans to give you hope and a future.

Prayer of a Worthy Lady

Father, you are awesome and wonderful. In your infinite wisdom you know my other side, more than anyone else. Forgive me for the times I have fallen into lustful thoughts and actions and disobeyed your instructions. Help me to be an example for others along the way. Thank you for all your blessings seen and unseen, for unmerited favor and mercy. Teach me your way and show me your path. Thank you for the blessing of marriage and family.

I ask in the name of the Yeshua the Christ

Diary 5
Letter 4: Walk in your Gift

There are many ways you can walk, but if you don't walk in your gift your path is crooked.
-Angela N. Brand

Dear Gifted

From a very young age you were singing in the church, you even led the song "Oh Happy Day" with the adult choir. That was a defining moment along your journey because someone recognized your gift. You were born a worshipper; your gift gives glory to God, and brings deliverance to the hearer's soul. Never take that gift for granted, it is not about you. Understand that the intersection of your gift (talent) and your passion is your purpose. Discover how to use your gift to help others.

We all have gifts and callings, give it your all. Be the best that you can be in all that you do. No matter how many times the door is shut or you are turned down, keep your head up and never stop trying. Note that you will sometimes be hated for your gift and your anointing. You will not understand why, it will make you want to leave the church, but never allow the jealousy of others to stifle your relationship with your God. In fact, allow the hurt and pain to make you stronger.

You tend to start then stop projects in life, never be a jack of all trades, and master of none. Stay focused on what is important, and

inish what you start, it is a critical life skill. To do your best, it is
mportant to hone in on your craft, study your gifts. Use every resource
o expand your knowledge, practice, and practice some more, and never
jive up.

Life will press you on every side; there will be good days and
bad days. Remember your attitude will determine your altitude. When
he storms of life are raging, go to the source of your peace. Worship!
Get into your quiet place and sit in the lap of the one who holds your
heart. Open your mouth and worship as you recall the toughest times in
your life, and count your blessings.

Prayer of the Gifted

Father, you are amazing. Thank you for the gifts and callings you have bestowed upon your children. Help me to use them for your Glory. At times I forget to count my blessings, I get caught up in the world, although you said be not conformed to this world, to be in the world but not of the world. Please remind me to approach your throne of grace. According to your word, I was created to worship you, and bring you glory. Help me to remember that when praises go up, blessings come down.

I ask in the name of the Yeshua the Christ

Letter 5: Heed the Prophetic

*Your prophetic word is to guide your path in God's will, heed them
and watch them manifest*
-Angela N. Brand

Dear Hearer of the Prophetic

Thank God for the spirit that is upon you, that is springing forth in a
new way and a new direction. Thank God for the mantle that He has
placed upon you, and for the clarity that he has given. Thank God that
He is healing all your wounds, for His namesake and for His Glory.
People look at you from the outside and always come to you, to be the
strong one, but God says now is the season that I am going to cradle
and comfort you. I am going to put you in the cave Adullum (hiding
place), and you are going to come out like David and his mighty men. I
had to hide you from some things for a season, but now when you come
out, this time, there will be no more setbacks! I curse every setback that
the enemy would try to use in your life; Glory be to the almighty God,
no more setbacks.

Don't let anyone tell you what you are not! Speak to the gifts,
activate the gifts even more, the prophetic and the divine intercessor,
because you are a Prayer Warrior! Don't back up and don't back down.
Yes, I am going to do a new thing even in your hands. Lay hands on
the sick, you shall, and they shall recover, because everything you have

been through, and the heart of compassion you have, God will use you to heal the sick and raise the dead. Everything you have been through, you should be very angry, but God has taught you how to love despite it all. With the gifts on the inside of you, lay hands, even on those who are mentally oppressed, bind it up, and it must flee at the word of God.

You have swords in your feet and a sword in your mouth which means you are dangerous in the spirit, which is why the enemy hates you so much. But he cannot stop this move of God. He has delayed some things, but God says, No More Delays, but manifestations for His glory, and even in the urgency of the hour – don't back up and don't back down!

People need the greatness that is on the inside of you. You are a warrior, be used in this season like never before. The blessings of the Lord will make you rich and add no sorrow. There is a release in the spirit, a financial release to manifest in your life, for the Glory of Almighty God. It is so, and it cannot, and shall not be otherwise. Touch not the unclean thing.

These words came from those who spoke over my life

Prayer of the Prophetic

Oh, Father how great thou art! When I received this prophetic message, my mind was amazed but at the same time I knew it to be true, for I have felt this in my spirit for a long time. In your presence there is fullness of joy and that is my dwelling place. Thank you for the gifts and callings. Use me for your Glory. Teach me to walk in your ultimate timing, without wavering to the left or to the right.

Our Father, which art in Heaven, Hallowed be thy name. Thy Kingdom come and thy will be done on earth as it is in Heaven. Give us this day our daily bread and forgive us our debts as we forgive our debtors. Lead us not into temptation but deliver us from evil. For thine is the Kingdom and the power and the Glory Forever!
I ask in the name of the Yeshua the Christ

Diary 6
Looking through the Window
Co-Author Sylvia Blue

Letter 1: Tap into the Confidence Within

There is true confidence lying dormant within each of us, it's our responsibly to awaken it and walk in the fullness thereof.
-Angela N. Brand

Dear Ms. Confidence,

 look at you now, showing all the confidence in the world, and thought about what it took for you to get to this point, what you had to go through, the cost you had to pay, and the times you cried yourself to sleep. I remember how other people always tried to knock your self-confidence, and for a while they succeeded, but then you took control of your life and walked into your destiny. I want you to know how very proud I am of you.

 There has always been a dream within you that God has purposely placed there that will change the lives of so many, but just know the enemy will try to snuff out that dream. That dream is your purpose; protect it with everything within you. The devil will use people that are close to you to try to kill that dream, but you can't let that happen. They will use words, lies, deceit, situations, and other tactics to try to make you doubt the dream that God has placed within you. You will be told that your dream will never happen or that you aren't good enough to accomplish such a thing, but you stand strong on that dream. Don't let anything shake you it's yours! God gave it to you and no one else. You must make sure that you never allow those words to linger in your spirit but use them as wind to increase the burning flame within you, to fuel your passion.

Feed your confidence, nurture it so that it won't turn into doubt, fear, and insecurities; speak life into yourself even if no one else does; talk to yourself in the mirror daily and speak affirmations to keep that confidence stirred up. Keep the dream visible; there will be times when you have no one to motivate or push you. Be your own motivator! No one can stop your dream from happening except for you! You have a Kingdom that lives in you that has already produced everything that you need to make the dream happen. You must pursue the dream, and it may seem way bigger than what you can do at times, but that's good; don't allow the size of the dream to scare you.

The bigger the dream, the more we know it can't happen without God's help, and we know that everything that God does is good, so allow Him to work through you. God has already placed a certain measure of confidence (faith) within you so there is no need to worry about not being properly equipped for the job. Remember, there is a Kingdom inside of you that will help you overcome any situation that may come up to throw you off track. It will get hard and you will want to give up but when it happens remember that God handpicked you to pursue that dream, not anyone else, which means that He trusts you and your abilities to accomplish the dream. You got this Girl! Your confidence will carry you to the end, tap into it! I'll see you on the other side of the manifestation of your dream.

Prayer of the Confidence Within

Dear Father,

I just want to thank you for placing the confidence in me to pursue my dreams and my purpose. I know because you gave it to me, it will surely come to pass. You didn't have to trust me with the dream, but you saw it for me to pursue it and for that I am forever grateful. Thank you, God, for the confidence not to give up, when it got rough or when the enemy attacked my dream. I know that there is greater in me than anything that may come up against me.

My confidence will fight for me, so Lord when I get weak in my flesh allow the Kingdom that lives in me to fight on my behalf. Let your Word be a refreshing spring to rejuvenate my spirit. Let your Word give me life and strength to keep going. Give me the strength to be unshakable and unmovable on this journey. Let no one break my spirit or my confidence. I know that you are faithful to your Word, so I'll have the confidence to stand on it no matter what may come to knock me off it. I know that on this journey you will lead and guide me on the path of my dream, you are a lamp unto my feet; I have the confidence that you will always be with me and that you will never leave me alone. I believe in you and I know that you believe in me. I will continue to praise you and give you the Glory because it belongs to you.
Amen!

Letter 2: Destroy the Curse before the Curse Destroys You

The curse only came to teach you how to break them and help others get free from it.
-Angela N. Brand

Dear Curse Slayer,

I know where you are right now, in the midst of an uncomfortable familiar place; you have been in this place before and it seems like you will never break free. You know that there must be something different, you can feel it deep within, but this is all that you've seen all your life; poverty, lack, insufficiency. Every time you think this is it, you are free now; BOOM....here comes another blow. Money seems to slip through your hands like hot butter; it's there one minute, the next minute you're seeking it out again. Listen girl, there is more, there is better. Jesus came so that we can have life and have it more abundantly; it belongs to you! It is your Birthright!

I know your mother suffered the same way, she settled for barely making it, so that was instilled in you. Your friends are experiencing the same thing and they are trying to make ends meet by any means necessary, no matter the costs. That's all you have been exposed to, and that's what they tell you; just settle and make enough just to get by. You've tried it, but you just can't get comfortable in that, it just doesn't eel right. You desire more, and you just can't let it go, your spirit knows here is more for you in this life.

I promise you that there is more! I have seen it, and I know that he cycle can be broken. I have suffered with going without, I know what it is like to be evicted out of a home, I know what it is to be without ights, and to even go without eating, because I had just enough for my kids to eat. I made a choice, that's all it took to rewrite everything I was aught. I decided not to pass that curse on to my kids; and to do that, I had to make a change. I will tell you that it's not easy, but you can do it, because I did. I started speaking life over my situation, and my situation started changing. It all started with me making up in my mind that I wanted better for myself and my kids. I didn't want them to experience what I had to experience. I made up in my mind that the curse ends with me.; that seems like a simple task, but when you have had something instilled in you for so long, that simple task took a lot of strength. You will have to go against everything that is familiar to you.

When lack started to creep in I spoke the opposite; I didn't allow what I saw with my natural eyes to cause me to accept anything less han what God said in his Word. In God's Word it says that it is He that gives us the power to get wealth but without wisdom, self-discipline, and ollowing Kingdom principles, there is no way that you can keep it. That s where a lot of people miss the mark; God must know that He can trust you with His riches, so you must abide by His principles. You must tithe and sow back into God's Kingdom. I know you are thinking to yourself, How can I tithe and sow when I can't even pay my bills or provide for myself?" Trust me, I was in the same place in my mind, I would start tithing faithfully then it would come times when I had to decide whether I would pay my tithes or pay my bills even though I didn't have enough. That was a test and I failed a couple of times, but after doing the same thing over and over then feeling guilty about not giving God what was due to Him, I decided-there goes that choice again-to trust God and allow Him to be my Provider.

That's when the curse broke! I finally got it; if I did it, then you can too; you will shed some tears and have some moments of doubts, but just know that whatever God does He can repeat it. God is not a *One Hit Wonder* at anything that He does; if He has done it before, He can surely do it again. So, tune out all the naysayers that tell you not to believe that mess; and God didn't tell you to do all that. Don't listen to the ones that tell you there is no such thing as a generational curse on your finances or a spirit of poverty. It is very much real, but you my dear are coming out! Move in silence and let them watch God bless your finances and the finances of the generations to come because of your strength and courage to be a Curse Slayer.

Prayer of a Curse Slayer

Dear Father,

I know that you have anointed me to be a Curse Slayer, and that you trust me to do just that. Thank you for that ability and the strength to trust you when my eyes see different. Thank you Oh, Lord for being a Way Maker, a Provider, and a Sustainer during my times of need. You have never let me down in any situation. I know that I can always count on you to make a way out of no way. You said in your Word, you would never leave me nor forsake me, because I am your child. Thank you God, for instilling your wisdom in me to be a good steward over the wealth you have released into my hands. God, I thank you for giving me the power to break the curse of poverty off my life and the lives of the generations to come. We will no longer be bound by the enemy, because we have found our freedom in your Kingdom. We will forever be grateful unto you for setting free our hearts and our minds. We shall continue to give you all the praise and the glory because it is due unto you!

Amen!

Letter 3: You Can Look Forward

When you keep hope alive, you can always look forward to what
God has in store for you.
-Angela N. Brand

Dear Young Prophet,

I know that there are some awkward, yet scary moments in your life,
where you see some things or have dreamt about someone and then it
happened. You can't explain it in words of how you knew or was even
able to see that thing ahead of time. This can be very scary if you don't
know what is going on, especially if it happens the exact way that
you've seen it. Let me just tell you, there is nothing wrong with you and
you are NOT crazy. You are actually very special; not everyone has this
gift and you have been specially chosen by God to be used in a unique
way. He (God) can trust you with this special gift; being able to see
things before they happen can have you feeling isolated because you
may not understand what is happening, and when you try to explain it
to people they don't understand. It is fine that they don't understand,
what really matters is, that you understand what is going on. This gift
that you have requires you to have a special relationship with God. He
trusts you, now you must trust Him. You must trust that God knows
what He is doing and follow His instructions.

And yes, this gift comes with some stipulations; one of the stipulations is that you can't live your life just any kind of way. What a great responsibility, right? I know people will always be watching and waiting for you to slip up, and the pressure of that will be great, but you can handle that. You won't fit in with a lot of people that you may try to hang with. You will feel out of place when you try to go places that you know you shouldn't be in. You just won't be able to be a part of the crowd no matter how hard you try. Having a prophetic gift where God allows you to look forward into the future is something that should be taken seriously. It will be hard at first and may even be frustrating at times, but trust me, once you get a full understanding of the gift you will be appreciative and honored to have been chosen for the tasks ahead. There will be many tears sown, but you will reap the blessings of being faithful to the gift.

I know that you didn't ask for it, and there will be many times when you want to return the gift back to the sender, but there will also be times you will be used to help someone else and it will be all worth it in the end. Now, I don't want you to get all scared and go hide when things are shown to you, you will have to get used to being different. Just remember that God has handpicked you because you are able to handle the task. He knows what He is doing and what lies ahead, and now you have a little sneak peek of that too.

Prayers to Look Forward

Dear Father,

I thank you for trusting me with the ability to look forward. I know everyone can't or won't understand, but as long as I know you are always with me, none of that matters. I see it as an honor to be able to be used in this capacity. I also know that it is a great responsibility, and because you chose me, I have no doubt that I can handle the task ahead. You are Alpha and Omega, the Beginning and the End, and you make no mistakes, so if you said it then I trust your word. Thank you for your strength in the times to come when the tasks are heavy and I am feeling weak. You said that your strength is made perfect in my weaknesses, so I know I will be able to complete the task.

Amen!

Diary 6
Letter 4: Fatherless Soul

Regardless of what father you don't have in the natural, there is always a Heavenly Father wanting to embrace you as His own.
-Angela N. Brand

Dear Fatherless Soul,

Words cannot explain the void that you feel, the emptiness within; the void of knowing one of the main people who should love and care for you just doesn't or at least that's how it feels. The questions that comes like, "What did I do wrong?", "Why doesn't he love me?", "Am I not even worthy of my father's love?", "What is wrong with me?" There are so many unspoken thoughts that are internalized that they come out as rage, isolation, and bitterness, just to name a few of emotions that overtake your life. The void of not having a father makes you doubt everything about yourself, and makes you question your worthiness.

Would you believe me if I said it will get better? So my dear, no more suppressing your hurt and no more smiling through the pain. You thought you was over it and wasn't searching for a replacement or someone else to fill that void, but I hate to tell you, that you are. You know that guy that has told you a few sweet words just to see how much he can get from you or that other guy that was showing you attention but has shifted his interest, they clearly aren't the ones that you should be with, but you are doing everything possible to get them to like you or to make them happy with you.

Yes girl, you are seeking for love to fill the void of your father not loving you; I know at the time it doesn't feel like that, but I am here to tell you what you are searching for, you will never find it in a man. Fathers were placed on this earth to love, protect, guide, and comfort their daughters, to teach them who they are, to demand respect for themselves, and not to settle, because they are worthy to be loved and treated well. When a father does not provide those things to their daughters, then a void is formed, and the only way to fill that void is with that fatherly love.

I know someone that doesn't mind stepping in, and will all that bad, turn into good; who, you ask? Well I have found someone that was looking for me. He has given me the love, comfort, and guidance that my father didn't provide. He has stepped in, and not only filled that void that I had, but He softened my heart so that I can freely love, without any reservations. He has come in to my life and has shown me who I am, and that I am worthy to be loved, not only with words but with actions. God is consistently in my life, and there is no part-time participation, He is always there. No empty promises, because He is the Promise Keeper. He is our Heavenly Father, and He will be everything that your father wasn't in your life. Everything that you are lacking He will provide because, you are His child, and that's what fathers do, they provide and protect; allow Him to be your Father.

Prayers from a Fatherless Soul

Dear Father,

Thank you for coming in and healing my heart; the love that you offer me cannot be explained, and I thank you for showing me that I can and deserve to be loved in this way. I know there are times when I don't feel like I deserve you, but you always show me that I am worthy. You are a mighty God, and no one can ever replace you in my life. You make the impossible, possible. I now know that you can be whatever I need you to be; there is no lack or insufficiency in you. Thank you for loving me, and for saving me from myself, O Mighty God.

Amen!

Letter 5: Flexin' In My Complexion

True Flexin comes when you are comfortable with everything about you, even the complexion God made you in. Embrace it, wear it, become it.
-Angela N. Brand

Dear Brown Girl,

I know that your complexion can be a touchy subject and it doesn't really get any better the older you get, but I just want to let you know that you are beautiful. Being dark skinned has been deemed as a bad thing in society and if you are dark skinned then you are way at the bottom of the totem pole. I am here to prove those people wrong, you are beautiful and wonderfully made, that's what the bible says, so who cares what they say. Who are they anyway? The darkness of your skin is criticized and talked about by people that feel threatened by you for one reason or another. You are criticized because of their insecurities. . Your self-esteem is beaten down daily, and you just want it to stop. They don't know any other way to attack you, so they attack your complexion and try to make the way God created you, to be a curse. I am here to tell you it is a lie; a lie that the devil created for you not to walk in your beauty and authority. The devil wants you to back down early by killing your confidence. If you allow him to make you feel like you are ugly or something is wrong with you, then you can't walk in your purpose to he fullest. He wants to kill and snatch the power that you possess, but don't fall for it, embrace your confidence.

Stand tall in your authority! Your power is in your voice; your power is in the confidence in which God created you to be. You are a threat to him, so he uses people to try to stop you. So today is the day that you embrace the way that God created you. You are beautiful just the way you are, don't alter anything. It's okay if you have long hair, short hair, natural hair or permed hair. Those things don't define you. If you believe what people say about you, then you won't want to be seen especially when God is pushing you out front. Everything God created is beautiful in its own way, which goes for you also. God made you beautiful in His own sight and you should agree. He makes no mistakes, and He didn't make one when He decided to create you. No more hiding in the crowd or feeling like someone else is better than you because their complexion may be lighter than yours. Who said that just because someone may be lighter in skin color that they are better than someone who may be darker? Who made that rule? It's time to break the rules and walk in your truth, and your truth is that you are fearfully and wonderfully made. Your truth is that you are beautiful and powerful! You are not the one with the issue, so lift your head up with confidence and keep Flexin' in Your Complexion.

Prayer of the Flexin

Dear Father,

I thank you for who you made me to be, it took time, but you showed me that I am beautiful just the way I am. My confidence has been lifted. My complexion doesn't define who I am, and you love me for me. I will walk in the authority that you have given me, and I won't allow the words of people to make me back down from who you called me to be. Thank you, Lord, for showing me my beauty and who I am in you.

Amen!

Diary 7
A Transformed Survivor
Co-Author Catherine Mitchell

Letter 1: A Mother's Betrayal

We will never understand the decisions our parent make or what they choose to stand
for, because we don't know their inward struggles or what troubles their heart.
                                                            -Angela N. Brand

Dear Cathy,

I remember when you came up with a different name, it was when you were about 10 years old, and you didn't like your real name, because you thought of it as a white girl name. I remember you thinking, "Why in the HELL did my mother named me a white girl's name, all my friends have normal black girl's name?" So, you came up with Cathy, short for Catherine, and from that point on, all your friends would call you Cathy. You are 15 years old, just starting high school at James Madison High School, in your freshman year. Cathy, do you remember being excited about the school, and joining the track team, as well as being part of the band as a flag girl? All your childhood friends attended, but you were also happy about meeting new people.

The beginning of the year started off great; but one day everything changed; your friends' attitude and behavior changed towards you. No one knew what was going on with you, you didn't know how to handle it, or who to trust with the situation at home. All kinds of thoughts kept running through your mind as a young girl, so you gnored the problem, and began coping with the pain by having sex, smoking marijuana, and hanging out late at night with your friends. You had no other way of dealing with being molested by your uncle and step-dad from the age of 5 to 13.

All this hurt, and the pain was very hard to deal with by yourself, you felt so alone, like no one cared about what happened to you. You were like, "ok, now they know what happened, is somebody going to jail or what?" You were waiting for your mom to come and talk to you about the situation; that day never came. It was the most disappointing feeling you have ever felt as a young girl. You thought either, she didn't care; she doesn't love you, or she just did not believe you. I know you were confused and didn't know how to respond to your mother, but it hurt you so deeply, because, of all the people that should have protected you, she didn't; "That's what mothers are for; protection, provision, and love, right?" You thought to yourself.

You are sitting in your room, in tears, so many emotions coming to the surface, such as pain, hurt and anger. You will never understand why she never came to talk to you, or even attempted to give you some comfort as a young girl who really needed her mother, OMG!! So, you just move on through life without any answers from her; what hurt the most, was that your mother stayed in the relationship; so, you lived in the home with the person who molested you. Wow, some love, huh? You felt your mom didn't give a damn about you or your sisters. How could she do this to us, we are her birth children, you felt she should not give birth to children if she were not going to be the best mother. You were so broken hearted because you adored your mother; she was everything to you as a young girl.

Psalms of a Betrayed Daughter

Lord I looked for you and could not find you, Lord you promise that you will never leave me or forsake me; Lord, where are you? I looked to the right and to the left and I could not find you. I feel betrayed by my mother, she was not there to protect me and rescue me. Lord I need you to be there for me when it seems the whole world is against me, help me God, I can't do this without you, help me God.

Letter 2: A Broken Teenager

The beauty of being broken is being put back together with the right pieces needed for your purpose.
-Angela N. Brand

Dear Broken Teenager

Cathy, why was such a thing allowed to happen to us; no justice was ever served for us. My heart was broken because she never brought it up at all, like never in life, she never addressed what those bastards did to us. Cathy you died on the inside, you pretended that everything was good with you, but you were hurting. I remember you crying many nights because you did not want to go home, you were not a happy young girl, instead you were a runaway, having sex before you were ready, and out in the club at 15 years old. You were crying for attention, but no one knew or understood your behavior, they just thought you were just being disobedient. You were disappointed with the entire family, everyone except your sisters. You started to hang with the wrong types of people in the streets, not going to school as you should, you did not even graduate or go to college like you always wanted to. What happen to your dreams of waiting to have sex until you were married, having children with your husband, living in a nice house with the white picket fence and the red door, you would imagine hat was every girl's dream. Right? You are a brave little girl just for trying to speak up and speak out about you being molested. Don't be too hard on yourself, because most girls would not have reported the abuse at all. So, wear your *badge of bravery* award with pride, I am very proud of you for not blaming yourself.

Cathy you are beautiful in every way, you are also very strong, I love you for who you are and what you have become. My advice to you would be finish school, get some support from individuals other than your family; like the counselors at school, since they have all the resources you needed to help you get through your situation at home. Never, ever be too scared to ask for help. Once you have gotten the help, go finish school and head to college, so you can live a good life, one without struggles. I just wanted to let you know that everything will be alright, hold your head up high and just keep pushing, associate with the right people who cares for you the most, who also have your back no matter what the circumstance. TD Jakes once said there are three types of friends one can have; he said *confidant, comrade, constituent,* people you know will fit into one of those categories. My advice to you little girl, is to release the hurt and the pain into the atmosphere, get counseling for it, so that it does not destroy your future. I know you wish you had the courage to confront your abusers and tell them how it made you feel, and how they destroyed your innocence.

Growing up was not an easy cake walk, it was hard trying to be a child like the other kids around you. Cathy express yourself every chance you get, don't worry about whose feelings are going to be hurt, or what others might say, let it out baby girl, tell the truth, put it in the open what everyone else want to sweep under the rug, you are done keeping any more family secrets.

Regardless of all you've gone through girl, you finish on top, standing with a bold, sweet, and pure heart. I guess that why you love children so much, even though you only had three of your own. Your desire to protect the innocence of children will become part of your purpose in life. Overall, you are so grateful for the forgiving heart God has given you, to forgive those who have wronged you. You are made very well by the creator, built to survive through child birth; if we can handle pain from having a baby, you can handle any and everything that tries to attack you. Cathy if you could change anything in life, you would change your whole childhood, because all the issues were left unanswered and unresolved. But in the end, Baby Girl, you made it, you survived it and you overcame it.

Love, Cathy

Prayer of Thanksgiving

Lord, I want to thank you for being there for me, protecting me and keeping me, even when I felt my life was going out of control. I kept asking you, where were you Lord, and sometimes I felt like I was alone, but when I looked back at it all, I realized you were always there, holding me up in the palm of your hands, and for that I am truly grateful.

In Jesus name,
Amen

Diary 7
Letter 3: Gracefully Broken

*When people try to break you and misuse you, it will be grace that
holds you together.
-Angela N. Brand*

Dear Gracefully Broken,

I know you have suffered 12 years-*that was 4380 days*-of emotional, physical,
mental, and verbal abuse, from the age of 25, at the hands of a man who said
he loved you. You felt disappointed with yourself as a woman and a mother of
3 children. But of course, you didn't really know what love was; sometimes we
think we know things just because we are grown and on our own, right? You
thought this was the perfect man, and even if someone were to tell you about
him being abusive, as young as you were, you wouldn't have listened anyway.

I do remember you being a quite young lady, who didn't really speak
much, only when being spoken to. Cathy you were the most beautiful woman I
know, I saw it every day when you looked in the mirror, and your smile was
amazing with that one dimple on the left cheek. You were also sassy, and
didn't take any crap from anyone; you were up front and spoke your mind
most of the time. I also believed that it was a little bit too much; I thought one
day your mouth would get you in trouble. Cathy, I know you remember
hearing the saying, that one day, you will meet your match, but of course you
thought it did not applied to you, right? The day came when you met *him*, he
said he would never put his hands on a woman, he even quoted a statement
from his mother, the quote was, "if you have to put your hands a woman, you

don't need to be with her, and if you find her cheating, she was never yours". I wish I could tell you that he would obey his mother quotes, because you took them to heart, believing that he will never hit you, or so you thought to yourself.

I want to tell you that some men do not really listen to their mothers about how to treat a woman. I could tell you that some man doesn't really mean what they say half the time, and maybe they say nice things just to get in the door. Cathy, I want to warn you that the first time you see the red flag of abuse you should leave, get out before you go deeper into something that was not good for you or your children.

I wanted to advise that there are different kinds of organizations that service victims of domestic abuse. But because of the lack of knowledge, you didn't know that help was out there for you, and if you would have been educated on the signs of abuse, there was no way you would have allowed such behavior to come into your life. Everything he said at the beginning was a lie; I wish I could tell you that you will never be abuse in your life, but according a statistic report, 1 in 4 women will be abused at least once in her lifetime. And every 90 seconds, a woman is being beaten by her partner that is very scary to you.

Prayer of the Gracefully Broken

Dear God, thank you for helping to put the broken pieces of my life back together again, only you could piece together all the parts of my shattered existence. Thank you, God, for being my Potter and for molding me into the queen I am today, without you, none of who I have become, would even be possible.

Amen

Diary 7
Letter 4: Errors of my Life

Regardless of what errors you make in life, you can always rewrite your story with the expected end that leads you to your purpose.
-Angela N. Brand

Dear, Errors of my life

One day about 18 years ago, in 2000 you found yourself in a 12 years abusive relationship; not knowing what you were getting into at the time. Cathy, to tell the truth you were too busy, worrying about being a single parent; and girl, you were just amaze at how fine and good looking your abuser was, with nice hazel eyes, washboard abs, and them lips...(lol) and his kind words at the beginning, you did not see any of the abuse that followed. If I can tell you one thing, it would be not to ever judge a man by his looks, any more. Just wait on the Lord, look at a man's heart from now on, that's how God judges, by our hearts, not our outward appearance. Many times, you wanted to have a happy and peaceful life with him, other times you dreamed of killing his *ASS*. Cathy, you seem to have lost your identity, so much so that you didn't recognize yourself anymore, it seems like you disappeared; where did you go Cathy? You were lost in the universe for 12 long years, not knowing how to respond to the threats, the cursing, and the beatings.

Cathy, I want to tell you that your abuser hurt you deeply inside and out, it never stopped, every single day you suffered a black eye, being choked, and dragged down the hallway of your house by your hair. I remember him threatening to put your ass in the hot fire place, all because you didn't answer the question he had asked, the way he wanted to hear it. Let me add just few more things you have gone through; the biting, being spit on. I wasn't sure if there was anything else this man could do to you next but kill you. And oh yeah, do not forget to mention he have called you stupid, made fun of you, making jokes and laughing at you, do remember the time he embarrassed you in front of his family, by asking you to read a word that was very difficult for you to pronounce. Girl, I know that hurt you mentally, even though you didn't show it, yes indeed, that really hurt your feelings. Your life was draining, you were depressed every day. It wasn't easy going to bed, not knowing if you would wake up to see your family or friends.

But today I want to tell you how proud I am of you and how far you came since your last fight before ending the relationship. You are pure, with a smile that the entire world can see when you enter a room, there is no more darkness. God has shined his light onto you; you are shining like the midnight star.

You allowed someone who said he loved you, to treat you as if your life didn't matter. I am here to give you a little encouragement and some advice as a gracefully broken survivor; *don't ever....ever...I mean ever* allow or accept any kind of behavior nor abuse from anyone especially if they claim to love you; love does not hurt, love is patient, love is kind, love respects, and protects, that is love.

Now let me tell you what love isn't; love does not envy, not easily angered, does not boast, and does not physically abuse you. So, if you happen to come across someone like him again, you already know how to handle that situation, call the police and get the hell man loves you with not just his words, but with his actions as well; look at how he talks to you or how he takes time out just to spend time with you, and how he respects you as a woman of God. Sit back and watch how he pays attention to your every need, see how he put your needs before his.

Cathy, there are so many ways to tell that a man truly loves you and want to be with you; this time you are going to take your time and wait on God to send your soul-mate. It's ok to be alone for a while, that way you can learn to love yourself and value who you are as a woman. Cathy, just take your time, there is no need to rush into a relationship. What I want you to do, is go on a few dates, you don't have to put all your eggs in one basket, something simple, just talk and enjoy food and conversation, nothing serious. Remember there are steps to take when getting into a relationship and finding your Boaz;

1. Get counseling and therapy to begin the healing process of old scars and wounds from previous relationships.

2. Embrace self-love and self-awareness that is important to keep track of, take time out for you, not for everyone else, just you and some nice relaxing music. This will help you learn things about yourself you didn't realize before, so now you know who you are, who you want to be and where you want to go.

3. The next step is to develop your purpose and give it your all, without doubt or fear; this will go a long way in many areas in your life.

4. Cathy, do not just let any man enter your life; you are a Queen who deserve to be treated like royalty, make sure he open doors for you, pull out your chair at a restaurant, if he does not, it is okay to remind him to.

5. And lastly, never judge a book by its cover, what looks good on the outside might not be good on the inside, so the next time he is around, start out. Cathy, you should also get a license to carry a gun, and take some type of self-defense class, just like Jennifer Lopez in the movie, *Enough*, she had enough of the abuse from her husband, and she was willing to fight and take her power back. Make sure you look into his heart, find a man who has morals, has potentials for the future, and one more thing, we don't want a broke or broken man next time.

You can see God's hand was on you the whole time you were going through those 12 years, and still to this day. He said he cares for you and loves you, without God guidance you would not have made it through that abusive relationship, and I'm so glad you did not marry him when he ask you to, the nerve of him even ask you after all the abuse. I know how much you loved him and you really wanted the relationship to work because you always see good in everybody, you believed in him more then you believed in yourself.

Cathy, you were hoping that one day God would change him, and he would start treating you better. Catherine (aka) Cathy, you just wanted to have your Happily Ever After, just like in the Fairy

Tales. You were wondering what was wrong with you, and why you could not have the same ending just like Cinderella did in the movies. I tell you what, your happy movie is still in progress, and has not been completed, your happy ending is just around the corner, so just be patient, because at the end of it all you'll be sitting on the couch eating popcorn and sipping on a bottle of water watching the ending of *A Transform Survivor*.

Cathy, I am here to tell you that your relationships will not be the last one that goes through trials and tribulation, you must go through life's journey, to get to the purpose and the plan that God has for your life. Girl this was school for you and God was your teacher, preparing you for the future, using you for His glory, to tell your story and to help other victims. It is the same as when you are going through high school, the teachers were there preparing you for college and the work world. It was all in God's plan; you did not understand why you were going through so much stress, now you know that God had it all in His hands.

Cathy, I see you now as beautiful as ever, strong, confident, with a glow all over your face, it shows even when you smile, that's something no one can take from you, the light that is shining on you and through you, my dear sister. You have so much more to offer the universe, more than you could even imagine. What you see now is only the beginning of God work, all you must do is keep your eyes on the path, despite of all the distractions that come along the way, you must hold on because the blessing is coming sooner than you think. I am so proud of you, of how you overcame the abuse and you are still standing, even when the battlefield got harder and rougher you did not quit on you, or your kids. I thank you for being so strong, confident, you believed in yourself. This shows your kids how strong of a woman you are, it doesn't matter how long it took you to leave the abusive relationship, it was the determination, the faith, and trust in God, which led you away from all that drama. After a while, you started to think to yourself, he didn't deserve your love, he didn't deserve you; you were in love, but you didn't get it in return.

But as time went on, you decided you needed to get assistance for your depression and abuse, which was the next best decision you could have ever made, getting the help you needed to recover from being in a domestic violence relationship for 12 years was key to your recovery. That was hell, but you made it out alive and well. Thank you, Cathy, for following the faith, and getting a fresh start at the age of 34. I remembered you saying to yourself, "Yeesss...Yes I am a free woman". That was the best feeling ever, it felt like a weight have been lifted off your shoulder. After a while, you started working on yourself, realizing that your unhappiness was not good for you or your children. I so grateful for your boldness and courage, stepping up to what you believe you deserved. I feel you should be given the bold and courage woman award.

What you have done, most women don't get the opportunity to come out alive. I want to let you know that there are so many women just like you that need your spirit of courage and faith; this is just the beginning for you, the world needs you to spread the word about domestic violence. It is important to know that women in every community world-wide will be asking for you to be interviewed on television shows and local radio station, so that they can hear your story. You just keep on advocating and speaking like you've been doing and watch how the goodness of God will lead you in the right path. Cathy, girl, you are on your way to success, what you have gone through was not in vain, but a plan of God. I want you to look at how many women will be looking at your bravery and your determination to empower themselves. Someday you will look back on all this and see it was well worth it, the physical, mental, verbal and emotional abuse, and see how you can use your story for the greater good, for the other victims and their family who suffer from losing a loved one due to domestic violence.

Prayer of Thanksgiving

Thank you, Jesus, for blessing me to survive the abuse; I'm grateful to you for protecting me and not allowing him to take my life. According to statistics, I should have died from the abuse, or end up in a mental institution, but your grace and mercies stepped in and kept me alive, and so I can truly say, that I am not a victim, but a Victor. I am victorious because of you God, I have a bright future, free of the shame and guilt, and most of all, free of my abuser.

Thank you, Jesus.

Letter 5: A Transformed Survivor

Your storm, abuse, trials and situations were not meant to break you, but to make you into A Transformed Survivor.
-Angela N. Brand

Dear Survivor

You are grateful to have the opportunity to service, speak and empower victims through their emotional wounds. Cathy, you deserve to be happy and what you went through with your abuser was not a reflection of who you are or what you are worth. Surviving domestic violence is a one day at a time process; believe that forgiveness is important in moving on, but not forgetting, because this has made you a stronger woman. Domestic violence survivors find strength and healing in sharing their story with others; your insight and inspiration will save many lives. You have been truly blessed by God all mighty, to be the Advocate, a Motivational Speaker, and the founder of F.A.R. Ministry.

This is something that you just don't hear enough about, life after the abuse, this can be a positive journey, but sometimes you feel like it's harder than the abuse. You are extremely thrilled to be writing about your life and what many other survivors go through but stay silent about. Many hearts will be touch and inspired by your bravery of speaking up and speaking out about domestic violence and being free from it. You are A Transform Survivor who sees life wide as the ocean, and high as the mountains, it is beautiful, and full of many opportunities; exploring the things around you as if it was your first time on an airplane or cruise ship.

The freedom to speak and go where you want to go without answering to anyone is exhilarating, you stand here a witness of a Transformed Survivor, your kids are doing well; your oldest son is training to go to the army, while your middle daughter is in college in Houston and your youngest daughter is in high school as a sophomore, running track. These kido's are your world, you'll do anything to provide, protect, and push them into their purpose. God couldn't have given you a better life than this one; I am so, so proud of you, and I have no regrets or shame on how your life evolved.

Every time you get the opportunity to share your story there is glow on your face, anyone can see it from a mile away, I'm excited about the next chapter in your life and who you get to meet, the places you will travel to. This wasn't a tragic situation, it was a blessing from God, who allowed you to live and be a witness for so many other victims of abuse. As a Transform Survivor, you will keep working on your goals and dreams. It Begins with You!

Prayer of Thanksgiving

Lord you are Alpha and Omega, the first and the last, without you there is no end and no beginning. You said in your Words that before you formed me, you knew me, you knew all the struggles, the pain and the abuse I would go through, and you stayed right beside me; covering me and making a way out of no way for me and my children. Thank you, God, for the opportunity to be a successful motivational speaker, and author, for it is through my story that others can be healed and delivered. I thank you for these blessings, in Jesus name I pray, Amen.

Diary 8
Transformed and Made New
Co-Author Spring Jackson

Letter 1: Sweet Warrior Princess

*Behind every queen there was a princess that didn't know a warrior was
on the inside of her.*
-Angela N. Brand

Hey Little Girl,

You are beautiful inside and out and you do not even know it. You are
the biggest ball of energy with sass, from the moment you could talk.
You advocate for yourself, those around you, and take no junk as little
as you are. You spoke your mind way before you could formulate real
sentences. Your family is always telling the story of a strong willed,
outspoken little busy body. What comes to mind is the one about you
walking around the house telling your only Aunt to "shut up." Where
did you come up with that one? Because it was so cute, and you were
that little, are the only things that saved your life. You leaped, jumped,
and hopped all the time and stayed in trouble because you could never
be still.

Your uncle called you "Action Jackson," and still does to this day,
because you whirled, twirled, spun and did pirouettes instead of
walking. Ironically, when you grew up you would come to command
children of the same age range to "WALK!" How you would giggle to
yourself remembering that it used to be the hardest thing for you to do,

but for safety's sake, you had to say it. No one gets hurt on your watch! A small smile would grace the corners of your lips as you watched for split seconds realizing your love for little people.

Can you remember back when you were about 3 or 4-year-old growing up in California? It was where you were first introduced to dance, and for a while, going to the dance studio was all you ever wanted to do. Although you have a love for your leotards and tutu's, you have the spirit of a tomboy. You were never allowed to choose what you wanted to wear, but you would rather be in shorts over a skirt and gym shoes over dress shoes any day; you are your own little Warrior Princess.

You have always had an inner toughness, not taking much from anybody. What about that time you hit your sister in the head with a bat? Yes, a bat...in the head! I could only imagine what was going through your head at that moment and then hers. She must have been trying to tell you what to do, at 3 years old; you were NOT having any of that! Somewhere later in life, your take no stuff attitude turns into takes everybody's stuff, and never say NO. Don't worry, years would go by, but you eventually regain the girl that you were always meant to be you absolutely will become the woman you are destined to be.

What I want to tell you is that your life will endure some things; hold on to that childlike toughness, and the ability to be honest with yourself and others if you can. My suggestion would be to stay as fun loving, energetic and whimsical, as the moments that you would take flight in dance. There will be times when you will become consumed with the issues of life. Listen to the voice inside you that has talked to you for as long and as far back as you can remember. It is the voice that told you to duck under the table during the earthquake; it is the voice that would not allow you to go in the store with your older cousins stealing at the 711. It is the voice that helped you have courage for the journey, and of Him, that will see you through.

You have an important call on your life and a special anointing. Stay young and innocent for as long as you can sweet girl. Because of that anointing, you are going to endure some things that will develop the Queen in you.

Sincerely,
Ma, Ma

Psalms of a Warrior Princess

Lord I thank you for the innocence of childhood, thank you for the family that I was privileged to be a part of. It may not always have been the best of times, but at times it was the best! I thank you for my experiences, and even for the things that you sheltered me from. You knew me before you formed me in the womb and for that I am grateful. You knew my end before my beginning and for that I praise you. I am destined for greatness, so I know that you have placed everything in me that I am going to need to fulfill my purpose in God.

Thank you for making me fearfully and wonderfully. I know that you have always talked to me, even when I was very little. I thank you for your love for me and staying close to me. I am so grateful for the gifts in me. To be able to dance, sing, write and display your loving kindness, are wonderful gifts. I can only hope that I do not take them my gifts for granted. I pray Father that, I can give you glory in some way through my gifts, and that it will show from my life.

In the name of Jesus,

Amen

Diary 8
Letter 2: Big Dreams...My First

Big dreams don't come to small thinkers. Real dreamers don't care how big the dreams are, they have the wisdom to take one idea at a time.
-Angela N. Brand

Dear Pretty Lady,

Life has presented some changes up to this point; you left your birthplace of California and moved to Chicago to live with your grandmother. Instead of shrinking in the room full of family and cousins, don't forget to continue to use your voice. Things in your life was ok, you are strong willed and determined. Instead of just you and your big sister, there is now a little brother and a school of cousins. You are the youngest girl almost all the time, but things will change again soon.

Moving out of your grandmother's house and in with your step dad wasn't so bad now was it? He posed as a decent influence. Do you remember when he asked you how you would find a solution to a problem that you didn't even have anything to do with? There must have been the most puzzled look on your face as you searched your brain trying to give him a suitable answer. He let you off the hook and told you, to be a part of the solution is to not contribute the problem in the first place. That conversation stuck with you throughout your life.

Do you remember your dreams of becoming a dancer or plans to be a journalist? You were going to dance at the Alvin Ailey American Dance Theatre or a journalist living in New York? Have you ever figured out how that was going to ever happen? Oh, my goodness, that piece of romance novel that you wrote that almost got you skinned! Never stop dreaming, writing or dancing no matter what life throws your way.

In two years you will move to Iowa, and there were several people that you meet that will leave a mark on your heart. Most of them are males because you were a tomboy and got along with the boys better than girls. You won't find out until later in life, which it is because you never really had a relationship with your own father. Being a girl without a personal relationship with her father around to give the least bit of guidance on how a girl should be treated and what to avoid, silently weighed heavy on you. You have no real idea how much it impacted you until much later.

There was even an opportunity to spend some time around your dad when he made it to Iowa. Although it didn't really make up for the time lost, it was nice none the less. You made a silent declaration that your children will never live without a father. Because of how important children are to you, and the gift of nurturing and advocating for children, you can see why you have always had this understanding that all children need their fathers.

You meet a young man your freshman year in high school that will change your life forever, around about your senior year. He gave you one of the best graduation gifts that anyone could give, your daughter. It won't be until your daughter is almost five that you become a single mother, but by then you realize that you can do it. Remember her, that feisty little warrior that didn't take any junk?

Turns out that life happened, and you have already taken some bumps and bruises, that tough little cookie persona, have begun to crumble, as you continued your day to day journey. Yet still, you have the heart of that warrior princess, and the tenacity of a determined mother, who you watched do it for years. Life hasn't seemingly prepared you for the things that your little girl will need from you as she grows up, but you will do the very best that you can.

Equipping her with things like her worth, self-esteem, confidence, how to save for her future, the importance of her education and overcoming the barriers that she may have to persevere, is where you feel you fell short. These are all things that you were never directly taught. Getting pregnant at seventeen and giving birth at eighteen could not have given you enough time to solidify the things you needed to teach her. The statement "It takes a village to raise a child," is the truest words no longer spoken. No matter, you push on and make the very best of what you have in your arsenal. You are beautiful and are shaping up to be a great mom.

Yours Truly,
Spring

My First Psalm

Thank you, God, for always being with me, that when my earthly parents were struggling to get through their trials of life, you were always there. Your Word says that you would never leave me or forsake me. I thank you for the people that have introduced me to you and will keep you are alive in my heart. Bless them well for their service, Father God.

Father, I pray that my daughter knows that she is the most beautiful thing that you have ever allowed me to create. Being the vessel that was chosen to bring her to earth is the first proudest moment that you ever graced me to experience, and I thank you for the assignment. She has taught me so much about myself and about the love that you placed in me for children. Although I know that she is ultimately your child, she is like me in so many ways. Thank you for giving me that joy, Lord God. I am hoping that I have passed down the best parts of me and her life will give you glory as well.

As a young mother, I did not ever have a christening or dedication for her, but I have always understood that she is your child, and like Hannah, I gave her back to you, God. I am just the vessel that was used to get her here on earth to fulfill your purpose for her life. Thank you for using me, In your son Jesus holy name. *Amen.*

Letter 3: The Love Affair…...My Everything

The Love Affair starts with you before you can make somebody else the love of your life. Never love everyone more than you love yourself.
-Angela N. Brand

Dear Miss Lady,

By this time in your life, you are realizing how naive to life you really are. You have looked for love and acceptance in all the wrong places. You have never really been close to females and don't have any examples of women lifting one another up. You have only seen the inside of a church a few times since moving to Iowa or been around many positive inspiring people in years. But your heart clings to the things that you learned in Sunday school. Left to defend for yourself even in your own mind, your dreams are gone, and your reality is all you have, and it starts to kick in fast. Somehow you keep moving on learning and growing into the woman you became.

Your mind is plagued with regret at times and you don't even notice that your self-esteem and eventually the security in who you are, walks away with each one of your failed attempts at relationships. You start spending hours in bars, starving for the attention; you somehow thought you needed from all the wrong people. Your bar hopping days landed you in a situation with a person that helped you make the mutual decision to abort a child. You came to terms with that decision as well and repented to God for not allowing His creation to come forth. The fact that you have a little girl, less than gainfully employed, inadequate childcare, no transportation, and no support system, feels like there is someone standing on your chest and you could barely breathe gasping for air at times. You wind up in legal trouble trying to work two jobs and relying on people who aren't family for help ran out quickly.

You walked into that bar and took a job not knowing that you would meet a man that would change the game and essentially the course of your history. God took your mess and used you one more time to bring forth his gift into this world. The cutest little boy you thought you'd ever see. He was the littlest butterball with the biggest cheeks. He will bring the father joy and glory as he walks out his purpose and destiny on earth.

You watched as your judgmental friends turned their backs and walked out of your life. Your decision to give your first son up for adoption was largely due to your instability and tough times, but you were also bound by the thoughts and whispers of others. Those who could or would not help, had so much opinion, and that stuck with you for too long in your life. Young lady, no matter what anyone says or ever does to you; you are the apple of God's eye. He loves the ground you walk on, and don't you ever forget it. It has been a rough road, and this is not the end, but you're going to make it. At this point in life, your self-esteem is shaken, and your confidence is all but shattered, but you come from strong women that modeled what it is to be a resilient woman.

It was a hard a decision that you made and yes you did some of t out of fear of the way people would treat you and what they would think of you having another child out of wedlock, with a separated but married man and no father to help raise him. As quiet as you tried to keep it, you and your oldest were being bounced around and evicted out of everywhere. As much as you will beat yourself over the next fifteen years, you must realize that it was a selfless act, and a decision that God used to birth your purpose.

The love for children you will discover is not comparable but immeasurable, and there is so much more to come for so many children because of the selfless act to give up yours. Although you suffered, you blessed the lives of a family and will leave a mark on the hearts of countless others. Well sweetheart, you have endured a lot of things in our 20's, but just know that you make it and you learn from all of it.
Love, Sprinyata

My Everything Psalm

Lord this been one of the toughest times in my life. There were real times of darkness and deep depression, but you brought me out of it all. I must take this time to thank you for your goodness. My words cannot express the love that you have shown. I have not even been to seek you. I have neglected you God, and I am sorry. I thank you for never straying from me, even when I am running from you. I thank you for still choosing to wake me up and start my day new. I can remember when I was a little girl and I went to church, and they said that your mercies are new each morning. I thank you for mercy and I thank you for grace.

I thank you God that even through some of the roughest of times that I have never attempted suicide or tried to harm myself or others. Lord, you are all I have turn to. I have looked for the love that I needed, lacked or lost in a man and I have come up short every time. God, I need you to wrap your arms around me, and surround me with people that won't take anything else but help me to get out of this place. Lord, I know that if I ask you for anything, and believe in your Son Jesus name, that you will do it for me. I believe you God!

Diary 8
Letter 4: Sanity Restored...My Last

There is nothing like your peace of mind and sanity; hold on to it for dear life,
because it will last through hard times
-Angela N. Brand

Dear Broken Woman,

Aaaaggghhhh! I can't take it," is what is screaming inside your head, as you lay there almost lifeless, hopeless; you can't cry, you don't move much, you barely eat, broken sleep...despair is settling in. How did you get here? What do you do now? You can barely care for your daughter. Your only interaction with her is when she needs to eat, bathe or get dressed for school. Thank God that she is such an independent little girl. She has been that way since she could form words. Her favorites were "Mootie" (a name she gave you for mom, when she was little) and I do it." You have managed to teach her a few things up until now, thank goodness for that!

There was a knock at your door; it took everything in you and all the yelling in the hallway, to get you up to answer the door. It was just one of several angels that randomly stopped by and interact with you and break the depression that you've slipped deep into. You know that you can't give up, you can't let go and you must keep going. Your decision has put you into such despair that you've never felt before. You have been through some things but not quite like this.

You have a little girl that still needs you and a little boy that you are confident will grow up better than you could provide at the time. You have made a very permanent decision from a temporary situation that will tear your heart in two, but don't worry, God will mend it. Just trust Him, you find out that He's pretty good like that. Little do you know that you will meet a man that will help you get out of your depression real soon.

One of these visitors would not just bang on your door but drag you out of the house, and make you walk for miles. Your journey ended up at a bar in the middle of the day time and she made you come inside and meet a friend of hers. Why Jesus? Thank you Jesus!!! You have another tiny little human that would literally give you back your sanity. You get it together quickly! Your ideals of having a family or two parent household are a thing of the past. You are in survival mode, and never letting another child get away from you, be harmed or not thrive in your care becomes your mission.

You have the closest bond with this little boy; he is somewhat a miracle baby to you because when it felt like you were just empty, void of real substance and value in this world, he gave your life new meaning. You played with him, hugged and spoiled him, more too somehow in your mind, make up for how you let go of your first-born son. It will never be the same, but you somehow make up for it by making sure that this little boy knows how much you love him. Ironically, no matter how hard you try, he will grow up thinking you love his big sister more than him.

You tell him how you purposely have never played favorites with your children, but he is not convinced. Then you finally find out that his assumption is since you had more pictures of her around and things that displayed her accomplishments. You just short of go off on him because he has no idea how hard it has been. You have sold everything but your tail trying to keep a roof over their heads and decent clothes on their backs. If he could understand a young mother that had to resort to selling drugs to pay bills, have transportation and feed her family.

You threw real live bricks at the penitentiary to have the basics but plenty of things that didn't even matter. If you knew then what you know now, you would have saved that money, purchased a house or invested some of it into something that would have brought residual income. Little did you know that the promises of God are yes and Amen. It will just take you some more time and some pruning to get you all He has for you. Keep living because what's coming for you is better than what's been.

With Gratitude,
Mootie

My Last Psalm

Thank you God, for keeping me in my right mind. The song says I never would have made it without you. I am a living testimony to the absolute truth in those words. I thank you so much for keeping me, making me, shaping me, molding me, and filling me through my experiences. I understand that it is all for your glory. You have shown me that you made me strong and resilient, and that I need to believe in myself and walk in that truth.

I thank you for using me to bring forth your blessings, so that you may be glorified. Thank you for being mindful of me, and you thought enough of your daughter to use me as a vessel to bring forth your children. I give each of these children back to you because I know that they are not mine. It was an honor to be used, and I pray that I will fulfill your request to train up your children in the way that they should go, so that when they are old they will not part from it. Thank you for using my experiences to show me what you have equipped me with. You knew my end before my beginning. The gift of nurturing, caring and advocating for children will be my portion.

In Jesus name.

Diary 8
Letter 5: Rise from the Ashes

Never underestimate what you think was burned in the fire. If you keep looking
you will see me Rise from the Ashes.
-Angela N. Brand

Dear Woman of God,

Over the years you have witnessed this passage but seen it a bit different. As it related to the two pairs of footprints in the sand, you think of Him as even more gracious. Your vivid imagination sees in the roughest of times when you wanted to lay down and quit, he doesn't just walk with you but scoops you up in his hands. As the sands of time dripped from his hands, you see Him symbolically picking you up, and the things that he needs to fall off, slide through his fingers.

You have seen this picture repeatedly played in your mind. The footprints in the sand are so different for you, but with your very active imagination, most things are. You are finally becoming okay with the fact that you are fearfully and wonderfully made. You are different and set apart for reasons that you are finally coming into view and you are embracing. It has taken you so much longer to realize the woman in you, largely because you have been so hardheaded. Life has been trying to teach you these lessons repeatedly, but like fine wine it takes time. Yes, you are laughing but it is so very serious. Your anointing, assignments and calling aren't for the weak or faint at heart. It took some time to get you to a place that you could push past your fears and see the things that God has for you!

Baby you are on your way. Don't you dare retreat now! There is no turning back. Even if there are things that you must face or do are uncomfortable. You do them scared, but you must do them. There are those that are watching you and waiting for you to win. Sure, there are plenty that would love to see you fail, but there are many more watching to see you do it, so that they will know that it is possible. Defeating your fears is conceivable; staying away from what will keep you stagnant and unable to grow and live your best life is possible. Go for it, overcome it, work it, and WIN!!! God has made you promises and there is no way to get close to them unless you show Him that you will do the work. Faith without work is dead. DO THE WORK!!! You can't just pray and trust, but you must also work toward your goal allowing Him to lead and guide you. The wonderful thing is that you will get there. It won't be much longer now.

No, "Life for you ain't been no crystal stair," as the poet Langston Hughes stated, in his poem, *Mother to Son;* however, you have taken strides, keep climbing and looking to the hills from which your help comes from. One of your favorite quotes will become; "And just as the Phoenix rose from the ashes, she too will rise. Returning from the flames, clothed in nothing but her strength, more beautiful than ever before." *-Shannen Heartzs.*

Suffering has changed you, but it has not crushed you, it has taken the things you thought you could not live without, and it has offered you something you may not have found this soon in your life if at all: You.

Miss Spring

Rise from the Ashes Psalm

Adonai, in the mighty name of Jesus, Aba Father I bask in the wonder of you, I worship you for who you are. You are El Shaddai, the Almighty God! Your name is mighty, you are worthy of all my praise, mighty are the works of your hands. You are the Alpha and Omega. You knew my end before my beginning and you never gave up on me, even when I was going to give up on myself. You are Jehovah Rapha, my healer. Your word says in Isaiah 53:5...But He was wounded for our transgressions; He was bruised for our iniquities; the chastisement for our peace was upon Him, and by His stripes we are healed. You sent your Son to die for us and with each stripe we are healed. You have healed my heart and restored my mind, and for that I am grateful. You are Jehovah Shalom; you have restored the peace that surpasses all understanding. With all that I have been through, I still have peace, I still have joy and a testimony that I will share with others to show you strong and mighty, and yet faithful.

I come humbly as I know how, bowed before you, thanking and praising you for your love. I thank you the opportunity to experience your grace. All I was ever required to do was lay my problems at your feet. According to Peter 5:7, your Word says, I am to cast my cares on you because you care for me. I thank you for maturity I have in you Father, in your Word and in your way. You have purposed me for such greatness and I decree and declare that I will fulfill my destiny and your plans for me. I will have everything that you say that I can have. I will do everything that you say that I can do and I will share my testimony with others to glorify and edify the Kingdom. Let your will be done for my life. In Your Son Jesus holy and majestic name. Amen

The Kingdom Delayed but not Denied
Co-Author Donna Figueroa

Diary 9
Letter 1: Letter to a Determined Princess

Determination does not have an age, it has an attitude, learn to develop it and it can take you to places you never thought you'd go.
-Angela N. Brand

Dear Princess,

At the age of eight you were already a determined soul; do you remember when you spent the summer with your grandparents in North Carolina? There will be specific jobs that you would be assigned; your male cousins would be allowed to drive the tractor. You would ask your grandfather to let you drive because you really wanted to learn how to drive too. He would say "No, driving a tractor is for boys, go and do thing that girls do." This will cause a list of emotions; you will feel dejected, less than the boys. All you wanted is equal treatment, driving the tractor looks like a gift, not a job. You will feel like your grandfather is a sexist, and you won't know the meaning of that word at the time, but you will be enlightened later in life.

While he is on an errand in town, you studied the gears, stick shifts and envision in your mind how you will drive the tractor. So, taking the next step, you took the key off the nail on the side of the barn, cranked up the tractor, and drove across the yard. Turn around, drive it back into the yard, pull the gear shift into reverse and back it up into the space under the shelter—without hitting anything!

Your grandfather was not amused, he looked you square in your eye and say "You are just like your mama–determined. Now, I'm going to whip your ass!" You gave you a whooping you will never forget. As you pondered what he meant by that statement, you asked your mother when she returned to pick you up. She would tell you that while she was learning how to drive, your grandfather would holler about her driving, he would say that she was not following his directions and it would make her nervous. So, later that same evening she stole his car and taught herself how to drive, you smiled, to yourself; well grandpa was right.

Princess, you would be so infatuated by the washing machine, you would stand and study how your grandmother would put the socks and other clothing through the roller to squeeze out the excess water. She repeatedly told you to stand back while she is working, you insisted that you were ready to work the machine, so you decided to practice so you can show her when she returned. You picked up a sock from the washer and proceeded to push it through the roller, but this time you will lay it on your hand and push your hand through the rollers.

You screamed in pain, at the top of your lungs! Your cousin ran in and unplugs the machine, but it keeps on running! By now, the roller was up to the middle of your hand. Your grandmother makes her way to the back porch, and finally turns the machine completely off, releases the roller and pulled your hand that was crushed. You never knew that the machine and the rollers were powered by two different plugs, the pressure of the rollers would burst your hand wide open, there was blood running everywhere.

Your grandma is Cherokee Indian; she didn't make frequent trips to the doctor unless it was necessary. She proceeded to rinse the blood off, pours Mercurochrome all over the wound and wraps it in gauze. She then tells you, "it will hurt for a while, now go sit down somewhere and think about what happens when you are disobedient. I should skin you alive; you got my pressure up high running to get to you." You would have the scars for the rest of your life and will continually be amazed at how the wound healed completely without stitches.

Many years later that same determination and inquisitive mind will be the fire that will place you in a high visibility position and cause you to be proficient at whatever you strive to do. You will take many classes; accept different positions, attempting to become a Contract Specialist. This professional general schedule series will have a potential to be promoted to the Senior Executive Level, which will be a much higher level of pay.

Princess, you will apply seven times and will be denied every time, management was still assigning you work for a Contract Specialist but would not promote you to that position. Being so overwhelmed and distracted, you will not hear your daughter say that she had left her jacket on the playground, and she was going back to get it. When you hear the door close you will pull off and leave her at the daycare. You would fuss about your workday while you are driving to school and will become angry that she does not respond. You will look in the rear-view mirror and see the back seat is empty. So, you turn around and go back to the daycare to find her being consoled by the teacher. As you approach them on the playground you hear the teacher say "See, I told you that she would come back for you."

Determined to know why you were not promoted, you scheduled an appointment with the selecting official to find out what is causing you not to be selected. During the meeting you will bring to her attention that you qualified as number one on the list every time. She will proceed to tell you "just because you are on the list does not mean that I have to select you. I am the director of this agency; you will never become a Contract Specialist. You dress as though you are a branch chief." Your response will be, that "your mentor told you to dress for the position that you want to have."

She will have no idea that everything you would wear to work is from the thrift store, but you select the best labels. As you leave the meeting feeling extremely defeated, you talked to the Lord, out loud. "Lord, this is not right. I am already doing the work of a specialist, four grades higher than what I am paid. I dragged my child to school with me 3 nights a week, to obtain a degree for a position that I may never obtain. How can I continue to tell my daughter to do her best, work hard and she will be rewarded and successful when she sees me continually being denied, what I worked so hard to obtain?"

You will see God move; one week later, the director's seven-year-old son will develop a rare disease, she would resign from the agency and the next day you were told that she selected you for the Contract Specialist position. You will be stunned because she has never showed any compassion, or decency towards you. The agency will try to force her to select another, but she knows of your work performance and will feel that you deserve to be promoted. After nineteen years of service, you will eventually leave the government and continue to work as a consultant where you will perform many years for various government agencies as a Contract Specialist subject matter expert. The benefaction you will bestow everywhere you consult would be reflected in this eloquent statement:

"My mission in life is not to merely survive, but to thrive; and to do so with some passion, some compassion, some humor, and some style."
~ Maya Angelou

Psalm of a Determined Worshipper

O Lord, My God, my protector and my keeper; you have opened many doors for me; you have been my battle ax when the enemy tried to ruin me. Every time he tried to sift me as wheat, you would show up and be Jehovah-Gador Milchamah, just like you did for David. You are the Lord, mighty in battle. I need this faith, not merely to win, but to be utterly victorious as befitting the sons and daughters of the Living God. I will place my faith in you. I will seek your face. I will choose to focus on the Kingdom of God, and your righteousness.

You have showed me how to just relax, and not be so preoccupied with getting, so I can respond to God's giving. I shall submerge my life in God-reality, God-initiative, and God-provisions. I can testify that if you give your entire attention to what God is doing right now, and don't get worked up about what may or may not happen tomorrow, God will help you deal with whatever life throws at you. Lord there is none like you, you take the time to come and see about me while you manage the universe. I heard the songwriter said, "How kind of God to think of me, to plan each step so patiently, to re-write dreams I thought I lost."

Bless Your Holy Name.

Letter 2: Dreams Set on High ✒

Always keep your dreams in high places. That's high thinking, high planning,
and high speaking.
-Angela N. Brand

Dear Princess,

Your aspirations of greatness would be crushed by your mother who thought that you should keep your head out of the clouds. You will choose the wrongs friends and do wrong things to be accepted; they would talk you into stealing clothes from the stores, smoking cigarettes and dating the bad boys. Cherry would be your best friend of the crew; she will become close to you like the sister that you wished you had.

One day she told you that we could be friends, but she was not allowed to hang out with the rest of the crew anymore. Her mother had heard the story that a member of the crew was caught stealing; you were both glad that you were not with them that day. Whew! Ya'll dodged the bullet that time! You would ask how you made the cut to still be friends, she would say it was because my mother met your mother and she knew you were different from the others.

You see Princess, you were raised in church, you were always singing in the choir, ushering, helping your mother, or disturbing the Pastor in his study asking too many questions. But, no matter what you asked he would answer your questions, he would seem to be amused that you were comfortable with coming to him. You would ask him, if he always wanted to be a Pastor? He would say, "No. God has a way of turning your life around." You'll say "Great! Then maybe I could still be a singer, live in a big house and travel the world, even though my mother says that it's stupid." She would say, "You need to get a job, like a good government job so that you can take care of yourself because you are not going to live forever. Get your head out of the clouds and stop dreaming all the time". You would walk away feeling dejected and lonely.

As you prayed about all these things, you wondered if God would even hear you. Beloved, He sits high in the heavens and looks down low on His children. He will tell you that all your experiences, The good, bad and ugly, qualifies you to help someone else. He will provide clear answers to all your questions, not exactly in the order that you ask, but He will answer none-the less.

At the age of thirty, you would finally get the courage to ask your mother why she never supported you like she did your sister. She looked you square in the eyes and tells you that she didn't because, "you didn't need it, and you are so much like me. Whatever is that you place your mind to do, you find some way to get it done. Your sister needed more help than you did. I'm sorry that you felt that I cared more for her than you. You are pushing to make your dreams happen, and you are a good mother".

You finally had that conversation with your brother to discuss how you felt inadequate because he was successful in everything that he pursued. He will let you know that his resentment towards you started before you were born. All his life he was an only child, and then you showed up; he was a senior in high school and wanted a car from your parents as a graduation gift. A month before graduation, he was informed that because you were coming, they were moving to a larger place. They could not afford to do both, so he had to do without a car, and to make things worse, he would be asked to babysit.

Two years later, you will be joined by a baby sister; he was so dissatisfied with having to share your parent's time and attention that he joined the military. Not to get away from you, as you thought, but to live his life. You will share how hard it was for you to follow in his footsteps, in your eyes, he was like Super-Man! He thought you were being treated like a princess, while he had to work for everything that he had. You both will be relieved from your conversation; you and your brother would be best friends and you would help each other through the difficult times. When he died, you will cherish those times and remember his wise words. You would not speak to your sister for ten years, but with the help of God, you eventually talked it out. She forgave you for not coming to her rescue; because you will not be ashamed to admit that you did not know what to do.

Princess, just as you would sit on the front porch for hours dreaming of spectacular people, places and things – the Lord would not only want your soul but would make you a Seer. He would show you those that need protection, and then place you in their path. You would pray for them and then follow the instructions that He gave you. You will date the wrong men and endured years of physical abuse; this will cause you to abort two babies so that you could finally be free from him. You would marry, only to endure more years of mental abuse and abandonment, the only good thing that you will receive from him is a beautiful, smart daughter. She would quickly transform into your body guard/warrior princess. She would look grown men in their eyes and tell them "If you can't talk nice to my mama, then you got to go!" Opening the front door, she will turn around and say, "You still here?" baffled, they will leave.

You would raise her to have her own relationship with the Lord, have an appreciation for the arts and take her on trips to various places around the world. She will go to college for criminal justice and become a younger version of you, to help the elderly and the homeless. You will be an amazing mom; you won't have to worry about her; she can cook, kick butt and take names, literally. You will understand that you are fearfully and wonderfully made by God; adversity will not sway you from speaking your truth, with power, you have the spirit of Harriet Tubman, as you assist in setting the captives free from the bondage of physical and mental abuse; you obtained the resources to help battered women obtain their freedom.

Your relationship with the Lord is strong; you can ask Him anything, like "Lord how are you going to send me a husband when you know that I don't like dating?" But God does all things well; he will send you to the other side of the world, have you walk into the room, let a man see you—and have him hear the Lord say, "That is your wife". He will follow you all night until he gets the nerve to say hello. He will court you long distance, meet you in a mutual location and ask you to marry him. The best part is that you still ate those potato chips, have big hips and big chunky legs, which he loves! Princess, you will smile every time you ate a chip remembering what your friend's mother told you; when she said you could not get a husband eating all these chips because it would make you fat, you can tell her how wrong she was.

Psalm of a Dreamer

Lord, if you dealt with me according to my sins instead of your grace, no one would be able to live and stand before you. I am so glad you loved me when I didn't even deserve to be loved. Thank God for Jesus Christ! You didn't erase my future because of my past. Thank you, Lord, you deserve every bit of my love. Thru the depression, being ashamed and continual mistakes that I've made – you have showed me that you can overturn, cancel and remove everything negative that came my way. You came to my rescue every time.

Some people wonder why I choose to worship God even in the worst times, but I learned we are not exempt from life troubles, so through it all I choose to praise the Lord, because I know he is still with me. He has made me glad; sometimes I just close my eyes and let my song of praise take my imagination away with it. I feel so special with you in my life, protecting me from what is to come into my life, by watching over my life. My past is behind me, bigger dreams are ahead of me.

Diary 9
Letter 3: Letter to a Music Lover

The love of music is being in tune with the rhythm of life.
-Angela N. Brand

Dear Princess,

You have been listening to music your whole life, your parents made sure that you had an appreciation for it, from the classics like Nat King Cole, The Crazy Cadillac's, to James Brown, Walter Hawkins, and James Cleveland. In the 60s, music will help you get through periods of loneliness and times when you don't feel pretty. With the hottest song on the radio, you will sing to the top of your lungs "Say it loud; I'm black and I'm proud!" You will see a television show where Mr. Brown performed in Africa and before he leaves the stage, he said "Cut of the lights and cause some more blackness!"

Every week there will be a new dance to go with the new record that you will just have to have – or you will die. Those were exciting times back then, awaiting James Brown, the Temptations or Stevie Wonder's new records to be played on the radio, and then rushing to the record store to buy the records. The 70s will be your most favorite era of music; the beat becomes funkier, the baseline will be louder, and the singing phrases will become syncopated and augmented–just truly original. Much like your parents, you will give your daughter a lesson in music. The lyrics will trip your daughter out, as she lives through her age of music appreciation. Besides, all her music genre sings about is sex, grabbing and shaking that booty. No yearning, no admiring from a distance, no passion—just a computerized beat with vulgar lyrics, specifically made with strip clubs in mind. This music has created a new genre called "trap music".

Music will also usher you into the presence of the Lord, at an early age, you will be a permanent fixture of the First Baptist Church of Marshall Heights. You see, your mother will make sure that everybody in her house goes to church. By the time that you are old enough, you find yourself singing in the junior choir, on the junior usher board, singing in the Easter plays and performing monologues in other productions. There is this one time that you were practicing your lines and you asked your mother for help, she gave the second line and then said "etcetera, etcetera" like Pharaoh in the 10 Commandments movie. So of course, being nervous as could be, you recited the exact same line loud and proud "etcetera, etcetera!" The audience screamed with laughter.

When you become older, gotten married and move out of your father's house you will discover the importance of prayer and the need for a real relationship with the Lord. It is praise and worship music where you will find solace and peace just knowing that God is nigh. Princess, there will be seasons where you will wonder if God exists. So, keep singing Princess, it is from your lips to God's ears that will hold you, keep you and most of all deliver you out of all your fears. Keep singing, until you hear the instructions to help set the captives free.

Keep singing, so He can give you a word to bless the people.

Song of a Worshipper

Lord, if someone asked how much you love me, I couldn't count the ways; your mercy endures forever. When I thought all was lost you reached down and rescued me. I will forever be grateful for how you conquered the grave for me. You wake me in the morning with a song flowing from mine heart, I sing praises unto you, Oh Lord, how great is my God.

He whispers softly in my ear, so I can hear Him that He is with me, so I should not be afraid. How great is my God? Blessed be your name, Oh Lord. I will sing praises unto, even walking through the desert. You have bedded me down in lush meadows; you find me quiet pools to drink from. True to your Word, you let me catch my breath and send me in the right direction. Your love chases after me, you are the everlasting God.

Letter 4: Letter to a Warrior Princess

Never underestimate the face of a princess, when you least expect it, the warrior will come out ready for battle.
-Angela N. Brand

Dear Princess,

You are a one of a kind, made by God; as His child, you too will become skilled in battle. Through mistreatment, isolation and persecution you will learn more about God. As you develop a deeper relationship with Him you will learn to lean on Him. Your faith will move His hands to cover and protect you. In time of trouble, He will hide you. This faith will cause you to become curious, and you will learn more about Him.

The more you learn about God the more you will be attacked by the enemy. For he knows the more you know about the things of God—the more powerful you will become. Princess, the more you learn about the elements of God, the more your faith grows. The more your faith grows, the more you learn about the gifts and talents that God has given you. Using these gifts will put the spotlight on you. You knew how to cover yourself and your family with the precious blood of Jesus.

Princess, before going to sleep, you will pray this: Lord, I cover myself and all my property with the blood of Jesus. I take authority over all demons of the night, bad dreams, nightmares, and anyone or anything trying to get into my dreams, and I command them to stay away. I ask for giant warring angels to protect me and my property as I sleep, through the night, in Jesus name. During the day, you will ask for a fiery wall of protection around you, in Jesus name.

Princess, don't be naïve, be as cunning as a fox, and harmless as a dove. Some people will challenge your motives; others will smear your reputation, just because you believe in God. Don't be upset when they haul you before the civil authorities; without knowing it, they've done you, and God, a favor. They give you a platform for preaching the Kingdom news! The right words will always be there; for the Spirit of the Lord, will supply the words. When people realize it is the living God you are presenting, they are going to turn on you, even people in your own family. There will be great irony here, expressing so much love and mercy, but experiencing so much hate! But you don't quit or cave in, it is all well worth it in the end. Your weeping may endure for the night, but joy comes in the morning. Know that before you've run out of options, God will come to the rescue. Princess, I am going to warn you that persecution is coming, but do not fear, for there is nothing covered that will not be revealed, and nothing hidden that will not be made known.

Eventually everything is going to be out in the open, and everyone will know how things really are, so don't hesitate to go public now. Don't be scared into silence by the threats of bullies. God is in control; he allowed the attacks in the first place. There's nothing they can do to your soul, save your fear for God, who holds your entire life, body and soul in His hands. Princess, you can do this just keeping your eyes on Jesus. So, no matter what it looks like, no matter what it feels like, whatever you must go through, know that you have the victory.

Princess, you are in good company; Jacob was a cheater; Peter had a temper; David had an affair; Noah got drunk; Jonah ran from God; Paul was a murderer; Miriam was a gossiper; Martha was a worrier; Sara was impatient; Elijah was moody; Moses stuttered; John was self-righteous; Naomi was a widow; Gideon and Thomas both doubted Jesus; Jeremiah was depressed and suicidal and Elijah was burned out. And yet God called these and more to lead his people out of something; that tells us one thing, that God is no respecter of persons.

Song of Praise from a Warrior Princess

No weapon formed against me shall prosper, for I am fit for the battle. God is my rescue during the storm, I will sing praises to Him, and find myself safe and saved. I cried out to you as the workers of evil are attempting to kill me, by drowning my soul with overwhelming pain and suffering. But you reached out and saved me. Lord, there is none like you, despite all the things I do; I can testify that you are always there. My enemies tried to hit me when I was down, but God blocked those fiery darts and kept me safe.

You rescued me from a backbiting people; you have made me a leader of people. People I'd never heard of, will serve me, my God set things right for me and shut down the people who talked about me. He pulled me from the grips of backbiters; the Lord lives and blessed be my rock; and let the God of my salvation be exalted. That's why I'm thanking you, God, that's why I'm singing praises to God, my King, for I am God's chosen, His anointed, both now and forever more.

Diary 9
Letter 5: Letter to a Chicago Chile

Chicago can represent a place of pain, but when you let go of the pain, it now can become a place of restoration.
-Angela N. Brand

Dear Princess

Don't dwell on the past; I remembered when you were molested by your father at an early age. When you became older, you will return to the place of affliction and let go of the pain. He will apologize to you for the hurt he caused; the two of you were finally able to have a daddy/daughter relationship. Princess, live life in the moment, build great confidence in yourself, after many years of pain, you will discover that self-love is very important. The ability of being able to love, show kindness and respect for others will be birthed out of this pain. Just smile girl, it will hurt at first, but trust the process, and remember that you are not alone.

Princess, you will be able to keep God first, and this is what prayer will do for you; he will give you the ability to forgive your father and take care of him until his last day. He would let you see your prayers answered, to finally meet your birth mother as an adult. He will allow you to lie on the beach watching his wondrous works. It is there that He will minister to you as only He can, as the waves came in and returned to the sea, so will your resentment and past hurt, be replaced with gratitude, forgiveness and peace. It is at that moment that you will know that God loves you and hears your prayers.

As I look into your eyes, they are deep as a river flowing with feelings far beyond your years. As you think about the goodness of Jesus and all that He has done for you, your eyes shine bright like the sun and twinkle like the stars. I am so glad that you have found your happy place.

This letter is dedicated to the lady in the airport.

Psalm of Worship from a Chicago Chile

Lord, where are you? I can't feel you here, it is dark and lonely here; I pray for peace, will it ever come? I look for my mother, but she is not here. Is she with you? I sing praises unto you for I have no one else I can tell how much I'm hurting. I sing praises unto you and you make mine heart glad.

I lift my eyes to the hills and you shower me with the light of the world. I want to thank you for shining your light on me. My eyes look up to the sky, as I worship you. You kept me from losing my mind. You helped forgive my past and look towards to my future. Your Word says, Judge not, lest you be judged", so I welcomed the mother that you returned to me, we cherish the time we have together. I want to thank you for hearing my cry.

Thank you for the love that is in my heart.
Amen

Diary 10
She was presented a Coat of many Colors
Co-Author Robin L. Johnson

Diary 10
Letter 1: The Seer

Never underestimate the sight power of a young Seer; as she ages, the power to see gets stronger each day
-Angela N. Brand

Hi Dear,

Robin, otherwise known as Puggie, hey love, I'm you wrapped in adult hood. WOW, what a tremendous journey ahead for the girl who adorns a coat of many colors. A girl with great imaginations, sight and unheard-of dreams, you will face many who desire to strip your coat. The Horror of demonic encounters, traps, empty promises, pitfalls and mental imprisonments, however you will triumphant and sit with many Kings.

I know dear, a Seer is a difficult responsibility at the tender age of five. However, Joseph, Jacob's son in Genesis chapter 37 had this awkward gift as well. I hope this will encourage you. Joseph had a dream, and when he told it to his brothers, and they hated him even more. He said to them, "Listen to this dream I had: We were binding sheaves of grain out in the field when suddenly my sheaf rose and stood upright, while your sheaves gathered around mine and bowed down to it." Gen 37:5-7 NIV.

Robin everyone won't like your prophetic ability, they'll rebuke you, shun you, mistakenly perceive you as arrogant. Robin, press forward that ability will bring you before kings like Joseph! Then the chief cupbearer said to Pharaoh, "Today I am reminded of my shortcomings. Pharaoh was once angry with his servants, and he imprisoned the chief baker in the house of the captain of the guard. Each of us had a dream the same night, and each dream had a meaning of its own. Now a young Hebrew was there with us, a servant of the captain of the guard. We told him our dreams, and he interpreted them for us, giving each man the interpretation of his dream. And things turned out exactly as he interpreted them to us: I was restored to my position, and the other man was impaled." So, Pharaoh sent for Joseph, and he was quickly brought from the dungeon. When he had shaved and changed his clothes, he came before Pharaoh. Pharaoh said to Joseph, "I had a dream, and no one can interpret it. But I have heard it said of you that when you hear a dream you can interpret it." "I cannot do it," Joseph replied to Pharaoh, "but God will give Pharaoh the answer he desires." Gen 41:9-16 NIV Robin, God will use your awkward undeserving gift for your good and His glory!

Love you forever,
Pastor Robin

Psalms of a Seer

Oh Lord, I don't understand, how this is a gift. Gifts should be wrapped n pretty bows, this gift makes my heart races, and it makes me feel award and odd. Please, I don't understand, take this gift away!

Letter 2: Overwhelming Fear

Fear is just a mechanism to paralyze your purpose and keep
you from moving forward
-Angela N. Brand

Hi Dear,

Robin, at this point you are a charismatic, pretty, fashionable young adolescent, clueless that there were underworld plots to kill your dreams! Literally, Satan invades your nights with visions of snakes, witches, dead people and voices. The girl with a great imagination, seer and unheard-of dreams, is now gripped with overwhelming fear. The horror of these demonic encounters has you trapped in terror. The bedroom is transformed nightly into an underground deep pit of pure hell, with sights and stench indescribable. Many nights you curled in a corner terrified, crying for morning daylight to appear. Robin, Joseph, overcomes a plot and a physical pit also, I hope this encourages you.

"...So, Joseph went after his brothers and found them near Dothan. But they saw him in the distance, and before he reached them, they plotted to kill him. "Here comes that dreamer!" they said to each other. "Come now, let's kill him and throw him into one of these cisterns/pits and say that a ferocious animal devoured him. Then we'll see what comes of his dreams." and they took him and threw him into the cistern. The cistern was empty; there was no water in it." Gen 37:17-24 NIV

Robin, your pit is spiritual, used to develop the inner spiritual warrior for where God is taking you. Like Joseph's pit experience was taking him somewhere, "Joseph was thirty years old when he entered the service of Pharaoh King of Egypt..." Gen 41:46 NIV

Love you forever,
Pastor Robin

Psalms from Overwhelming Fear

What love is this that leaves me in the bottomless pit? You left me surrounded by snakes, voices that haunted me. Giant creatures who threatened my life. I'm gripped with fear! What kind of love is this?

Letter 3: Surrounded by Scoffers

No matter who mocks you or come against you, God will always be your defense.
-Angela Brand

Hi Dear,

Robin, you were a high school drop out with a GED, a young mom of two small kids, a young woman with slight optimism and no longer a dreamer. Now, you feel the pull to serve God's person which was humbling and honorable at the same time, however you are hesitant. The girl who had a great imagination, seer of unheard-of dreams at this point, faced many failures, horror of demonic encounters, traps, and pitfalls. You would take a leap of faith and unveil yourself to believe again, not knowing there were scoffers in the religious institution. People, who would jeer, mock, give empty promises, lie and remind you that you are uneducated.

Robin, remember Joseph, he overcame jeers, mockery, and false character assault, I hope this encourages you. "So, when the Midianite merchants came by, his brothers pulled Joseph up out of the cistern and sold him for twenty shekels of silver to the Ishmaelites, who took him to Egypt. Meanwhile, the Midianites sold Joseph in Egypt to

Potiphar, one of Pharaoh's officials, the captain of the guard." Gen 37:28, 36 NIV

Now Joseph was well-built and handsome, and after a while his master's wife took notice of Joseph and said, "Come to bed with me!" But he refused. "With me in charge," he told her, "my master does not concern himself with anything in the house; everything he owns he has entrusted to my care. No one is greater in this house than I am. My master has withheld nothing from me except you because you are his wife. How then could I do such a wicked thing and sin against God?" And though she spoke to Joseph day after day, he refused to go to bed with her or even be with her. One day he went into the house to attend to his duties, and none of the household servants was inside. She caught him by his cloak and said, "Come to bed with me!" But he left his cloak in her hand and ran out of the house. When she saw that he had left his cloak in her hand and had run out of the house, she called her household servants. "Look," she said to them, "this Hebrew has been brought to us to make fun of us! He came in here to sleep with me, but I screamed. When he heard me scream for help, he left his cloak beside me and ran out of the house." She kept his cloak beside her until his master came home. Then she told him this story: "That Hebrew slave you brought us came to me to make fun of me. But as soon as I screamed for help, he left his cloak beside me and ran out of the house. Gen 39:18 NIV

Robin, the liars, those spewing false character assault and the religious scoffers are only a test to rob you of the greatness. Like

Joseph you'll be entrusted with much. "So Pharaoh said to Joseph, "I hereby put you in charge of the whole land of Egypt." Gen 41:41 NIV

Love you forever, Pastor Robin

Letter 4: Betrayed

Betrayal is a sign that you are on right path and the people who betrayed you was used to push you to your destiny.
-Angela N. Brand

Hi Dear,

Robin, you are now middle aged, you have overcome many obstacles and health challenges as a mom and a minister. Yet nothing prepared for the utter disappointment inflicted by whom you serve. You love to serve people through your ministry, and that same ministry will bring healing, prophetic revelation, imparts spiritually and practical resource too many lives. However, those very individuals you give unselfishly to, will be unpredictable, they'll try to sabotage you, leaving you mentally imprisoned. This will cause you to question yourself, if you are cut out for this, but don't you dare stop, keep pushing.

You were a wife who loves to serve her husband, but the love was not given back to you. Nearly 20 years of marriage went down the drain, as the charismatic, pretty, fashionable and intelligent woman to the world was not good enough for your spouse. Empty promises to be faithful, ended in heartbreak with every unveiled side chick who claimed she was pregnant by your spouse, every rude woman calling on the phone, finding texts, pictures, video's and/or receipts. You'll be divorced, abandoned, left for dead by your spouse, however you will survive.

Robin, Joseph serves many, receives empty promises and mental imprisonments. I hope this encourages you. "After they had been in custody for some time, each of the two; cupbearer and the baker of the king of Egypt, who were being held in prison, had a dream that same night, and each dream had a meaning of its own. When Joseph came to them the next morning, he saw that they were dejected. So, he asked Pharaoh's officials who were in custody with him in his master's house, "Why do you look so sad today?" "We both had dreams," they answered, "but there is no one to interpret them." Then Joseph said to them, "Do not interpretations belong to God? Tell me your dreams." So, the chief cupbearer told Joseph his dream... Joseph said to him, "The three branches are three days. Within three days Pharaoh will lift your head and restore you to your position and you will put Pharaoh's cup in his hand, just as you used to do when you were his cupbearer. But when all goes well with you, remember me and show me kindness; mention me to Pharaoh and get me out of this prison. Gen 40:5-14 NIV When the chief baker saw that Joseph had given a favorable interpretation, he said to Joseph, "I too had a dream, on my head were three baskets of bread. In the top basket were all kinds of baked goods for Pharaoh, but the birds were eating them out of the basket on my head." "This is what it means," Joseph said..." Gen 40:16-18 .

Robin, the utter disappointment inflicted by the people whom you served, is an indication of the great responsibility and reward God has for you. Like Joseph, God will cause someone to remember you.

"Then the chief cupbearer said to Pharaoh, "Today I am reminded of my shortcomings. There was a young Hebrew that was there with us, a servant of the captain of the guard. We told him our dreams, and he interpreted them for us, giving each man the interpretation of his dream. And things turned out exactly as he interpreted them to us: I was restored to my position, and the other man was impaled."

Love you forever,
Pastor Robin

Diary 10
Letter 5: Queen of Great Influence

A true Queen always use her influence to empower the people around her to become the best version of themselves in spite their struggles.
-Angela N. Brand

Hi Dear,

Robin, the girl who adorns a coat of many colors, your colorful coat represents your dynamic nuances; the spiritual, mental, physical, and emotional you, along with the multi facet journey of every hill, valley and pitfall experiences is something will bring unimaginable strength. You will discover each demonic encounter, trap, and empty promises, will mold you into a Queen of great influence. Joseph, a colorful gifted masterpiece, knew not the tremendous cost, nor was he fully aware of his colorful purpose that would subject him to haters and spectators.

"Now Jacob loved Joseph more than all his children, because he was the son of his old age; and he made him a distinctive multi-colored tunic. His brothers saw that their father loved Joseph more than all of them, so they hated him and could not find it within themselves to speak to him on friendly terms. "Genesis 37:3-4 AMPV

Robin, your colorful coat will be stripped, and many will drop you, but hold steadfast. "So, when Joseph came to his brothers, they stripped him of his robe-the ornate robe he was wearing, and they took him and threw him into the cistern. The cistern was empty; there was no water in it."

Cry no more, you will be temporarily dropped and stripped; only to permanently conquer, thrive and reign! "The plan seemed good to Pharaoh and to all his officials. So, Pharaoh asked them, "Can we find anyone like this man, one in whom the spirit of God dwells?" Then Pharaoh said to Joseph, "Since God has made all this known to you, there is no one so discerning and wise as you. You shall oversee my palace, and all my people are to submit to your orders. Only with respect to the throne will I be greater than you." Gen 41:37-40 NIV

Robin, the girl who is adorns a coat of many colors will have it snatched off you; don't worry, in full womanhood you'll be wearing royal robes as Queen! "Then Pharaoh took his signet ring from his finger and put it on Joseph's finger. He dressed him in robes of fine linen and put a gold chain around his neck. He had him ride in a chariot as his second-in-command, and people shouted before him, "Make way!" Thus, he put him in charge of the whole land of Egypt." Gen 41:42-43 NIV

Queen you are Love you forever!
Pastor Robin

Psalm of a Queen with Influence

Lord I thank you for every pitfall, disappointment, and setback that sculptured my position and defined my queenly influence!

To: My God parents '19"

Thanks For All that you do for my Family. God is turly with you walk in Freedom and Power !! :)

Diary 11
Broken to Forgive
Co-Author JaQuita Jackson, MBA

Diary 11
Letter 1: Where Are You?

Life seems empty without the nurturing love of a mother. But embrace and nurture one's self you will never yearn for it again.
-Angela N. Brand

Dear Little J

As you searched and searched for that mother you needed, you could not find her. Being raise by your grandmother was all well and good, but it is nothing like having your mother that birthed you, being a part of every great moment you achieved. Watching your friends have mother/daughter days together was tough; having that connection where you can share your deepest feelings, is something that you always wanted. You ask yourself every day, if you were a mistake; you prayed that your mother would be right by your side, but God saw otherwise.

I remembered as a young child, when you tried to give your mother a hug, and she pushed you off her; and asked you, "Why you were hugging me?" You thought to yourself as a young little girl, "What was I supposed to do?" Now that you are older, you ask yourself if there was anything in your childhood that brought you to this point. It hurt you when she said that to you; to this day you are afraid to even reach for a hug. Hugs are needed to show that you care, that's what you thought as a young child.

As the search continued, you ran into some hiccups, you wondered if you had self-worth. You began to tell yourself that you were not beautiful, and no one would want you because of your flaws. As you looked at yourself in the mirror, you began to pick out every little thing that you could find wrong about yourself. You needed the validation from your mother; just for her to tell you that you were wanted, would have meant the world to you, but she just wouldn't give you the validation needed as her daughter.

So the search continued to find the mother you never had. You begin to seek love and comfort from other women that came across your path, not knowing all God wanted you to do is trust in Him and allow Him to make that connection you were longing for. If your mother was more active in your life, you would not have tried to look for that type of affirmation in others. Now you begin to live the life of pleasing everyone else, so that you can be accepted. That is not what God wanted for you. He wants you to be liberated, to live and fulfill His will.

You are a mother now, and you will not let the same mistake happen with your three children. You have learned to love no matter what the situation is. When your children came of age, you reminded them of what happened to you, you love and hug on them, as much as you can, so that one day when you are older you will not be forgotten once again. You have learned it is important to show love and affection to your children, so they won't look for it in other things and people like you did. I am proud you being a great example of showing love through affection to your family. You are creating a legacy of love by showing them what motherhood and true connection of family looks like.

Sincerely.
Yours Truly.

Psalm of a Daughter

Lord, I thank you for not letting me lose myself or my mind when searching for my mother, thank you for helping me to come to the realization that all I needed was you. Thank you, for allowing me to see that if people don't want to be part of my life, I can be okay to stand on my own because you are always with me, upholding me with your right hand, and for that I am truly grateful.

Diary 11
Letter 2: While I Wait

God teaches us while we wait, that He is the only source to fill the void of life.
-Angela N. Brand

Dear Lady J,

You are sitting at the window waiting for your daddy to come pick you up, wondering what exciting fun he had in store for you.. As the seconds and minutes passed by, you began to feel a trembling inside, as the tears fall down your face from disappointment. "Lord, why?" As you grow older, the little girl inside still longed for a relationship with her daddy. There was a bond that was missing because you wanted him to be near. There was a love inside your heart, a never-ending love.

Although your love for your father was sincere, your family aimed to dismantle this image with negative words you would never believe. The pain and sorrow you felt, pushed you to believe this process was happening for a reason. There were times when you broke down and cried. You learned to call on upon the Lord knowing He new what to do to ease your burden. The day of your salvation was a wonderful feeling, when Jesus came to fill that void that was missing.

As you allowed the Lord to fill the void in your life of not having your father, you began to tell yourself, that you should talk to your father about how you felt. As this day came, you shared your thoughts and feelings, but you didn't know what his reactions would be; it turned out well. As the pain and sorrow of your hurt was release from your mind, happiness and joy begin to give you hope. You were glad to share your heart with your daddy at that moment. The conversation needed to be done sooner than later for the healing to begin. When you started over, you knew you would spend time with each other, and would share some laughs together. You knew your happiness would come back again. Now that you are older and understand things more, you wanted to thank God for this reconciliation.

Watching girls with their father taking walks together was hard for you to see, wishing it was you and your father taking walks together with him being gone, you have no one to walk and share happiness with. What am I to do, were your thoughts. You have no one to kiss you on your fore head and tell you they love you. But you understand that when God calls you home, you must go. You saw him touched many lives, so you made a vow to yourself that you would do the same. In his passing, he taught you that leaving a legacy is the most important thing in your life; especially for your children. Since the time he departed, a lot has changed. You begin to trust God to fill every void that has been missing in your life. Now while you wait, your journey is different, you are not only waiting to see him again, you are waiting to be with your heavenly father. The one that you know for sure who can take care of you, when all else fail. On this you have vowed to the Lord that you will walk in His will, until you meet again. "I love you, daddy, and I pray you felt the same way too."

Just by watching your story unfold you have blossom into a beautiful strong woman that is creating a pathway for others who have felt the same way you did. You are now able to help others deal with filling voids in their lives.

Sincerely, Yours Truly

Psalm of a Waiter

God, I thank you for returning my father to me, so that I could experience the peace, joy and love, I so desperately needed and wanted I thank you for allowing him to fill the void that was left when my mother rejected me. I thank you for letting me feel your love, even in those dark moments, when you called him home, you were with me, drying my tears and healing my broken heart, for that I will forever be grateful.

Diary 11
Letter 3: My Life Changing Moment

God knows what we need, who we need and when we need it to bring us to the defining moment to bring us back to Him.
-Angela N. Brand

Dear Lady J,

When you came to Christ on November 23, 2003, it was a life changing experience. The night, before you were in a teen club dancing with some friends, you heard a small still voice in your ear and no one was around you. It said, "Why are you here?" You heard it about three times. So you got your friends and told them you were ready to go home. You went home and fell asleep. The next morning your grandmother woke you up to asked you whose church you wanted to attend that day, her church or your aunt's church. Your grandmother disliked your aunt's church, you were very surprised and didn't ask any questions, you just got up and went. This was all God; you didn't have any dresses or dress pants at the time, so you went to find the best jeans you could. When you got there, you sat at the back of the church, with your arms folded, and watched the entire service, everyone was shouting, and praising God, and you wanted to do that too. You sat there and listen to the sermon, and when they offered prayer you went up there and told them you wanted to receive the Holy Ghost. So, they begin to pray for you.

and you fell to your knees, and the presence of the Lord came over you, and you begin praising God and speaking in tongues.

You knew you were a changed person after that day; when your friends at school saw the change in you and asked what happened. You told them that you were free because that's how you were feeling at the time. You were walking around the school with a Bible in your hand all day; you took it everywhere you went, even when you went on road trips. It was an exciting time for you because you were thirsting for God's Word. You had many circumstances that came your way at the age of 17 years old.

One day a friend of yours came to your house and tried to kill himself with a knife from your kitchen drawer. You kept talking to him and tried to get him to relax, so that he wouldn't do it. Let me remind you, you had just received salvation, and was a babe in Christ; this happened a week later. With God's help, you kept your friend from harming himself further by staying at your house. You cried because you didn't know what to do. God used you to talk to him, which is when you knew, you were special in God's eyes.

Sincerely,
Yours Truly

A Psalm to the Lord

God, I thank you for letting me know how special I am in your eyes, so that I believe I can come through every situation in my life. If it wasn't for you God, I don't know where I would be. God, I thank you for teaching me patience, to persevere, thank you, that when I am weak, you give me your strength, thank you, God

Letter 4: The Power of Endurance

Victory comes to the person who is willing to believe in one's self and endure
whatever it takes it get what they want
-Angela N. Brand

Dear Lady J,

It has been a long road since the time you reached 18 years; what a journey it has been, where should I start? Here goes everything; you thought you were about to leave high school as *B* student, but there was one obstacle that stood in your way of graduation, and the *Georgia High School Graduation Test*, which by the way, is not in existence anymore. This is one test you thought would never leave your life. After taking the test 13 times, two times you made a 499, when you needed a passing score of 500. You were determined that you would keep going no matter how long it would take you to pass this test.

Nine months after graduating from school, you still did not have your high school diploma, many people began to talk in your ear and told you that you should give up on that test and go take the GED. You told them that you were just not a good test taker, it was not the test. You thought to yourself, why should you pay for the GED, when you can get your high school diploma for free? That just did not make sense to you. Since that time in your life, you kept listening to what people hought about you, and not about what you thought. So, you listened to he Nay Sayers, and went and took the GED, and failed it by one point. You told yourself you will not pay another $50 to fail, when you could have failed for free.

You were determined that you will get your high school diploma; so you decided to step out on faith, and write a letter to the people that were in charge, and even had the Church Administrator write a letter of recommendation to say how you deserved to get a passing score, and requested that your scores be waived because of the one point. You prayed over the letter then mailed it off; a few weeks later, you received a letter in the mail stating that they would waive the science test, but not the social studies test. With tears running down your face, you were not sure where to go from the disappointment. You were tired of this test holding you back, but you had no intention of giving up.

You began to feel that you were an outcast. All your friends had moved on and you felt stuck. You began giving a $25.00 seed offering, and writing on the back of the envelope, "I will pass this test". You started studying as hard as you could; you had your out of town friends on the phone with you while you studied. The day before you went to take the test again, you mailed another letter stating the reasons why you should get the test waived. As you took the test, you just knew you had passed it, because everything you studied the night before was on the test, you knew then God was with you.

While waiting patiently for the test results to come in, and the response to waiver, the letter came back first. You picked up the letter, held it in the air and thought, no matter what, you will keep pushing. You were shaking so badly, you were in tears before you even opened it. You opened it just a little bit and read it, it stated that they had granted your request to waive your score, and that you may call your high school counselor to receive your high school diploma. With tears rolling down your face, you said, "I got it, thank you, Jesus!" That's not all, you called the counselor to set up a time to pick up the diploma, she said she was glad you called because the test results had arrived the previous day, and that you could come and get it the next day. So, you did, and when you got there, she looked at your scores, and saw where you had passed the test. You thought, "Wow, God has been good to me, now I can begin my life, and pursue my dreams, like I always wanted."

I wanted to let you know that you have come a mighty long way, and I know that that God is with you because you have endured a lot since then. You have completed your BA in Religious Studies and now you have your MBA. Through all of that, you got married and had three beautiful children. There has never been a time where I have thought you were a failure. You have pushed through every trial that has been placed before you. God has truly shown you His love, despite of what you have been through. Keep pushing, because God has a lot in store for you. Many doors will open for you because of what you have been going through.

Yours Truly

Psalms of the one who Endures

God, I want to take this time to tell you how grateful I am for all you have done for me; thank you God for helping me through my many test and trials that I had to face in the process of becoming an adult. You taught me to trust you in all things and you will see me through. You are my everlasting Father, my Prince of peace, my Lord and my God. Amen

Letter 5: I Love Him No Matter What

Most people give up on love, but it's the one who endures it get the rewards of it.
-Angela N. Brand

Dear Spiritual Warrior

Remember when you were with him, how you felt peace and love; just one kiss from him transferred you to another dimension. Remember how you felt when he told you that nothing else mattered but you; through good or bad, he is always there, believes in you, making you feel that together you can conquer any obstacle that came your way. He was the wind beneath your wings and the love of your life. With him you feel safe and protected; when he holds you in his arms, nothing else mattered, whether you are happy or sad, he is still there shielding you from the pain. Remember how he gave you strength when you were weak, when nothing else mattered? He is the love of your life; this is what you needed to go back to, when it felt like all else failed...the love of your life, was something you had to fall back on when *he* failed you.

Remember the first time you laid eyes on your love? It was like a dream came true; not knowing anything about him. "Who is this man," you thought to yourself, he is tall, brown skin and handsome. A still small voice came to your ear and said, "You are here to help him get to his destiny." Then you said to yourself, "Are you sure, I do not think I'm ready?" God said, "Trust me." That is just what you did, trusted God.

While getting to know him, it was hard for you to decide if this should go further than friendship, you wondered if you were ready to become involved with him and dealing with his children's mother. You moved past that and allowed him to be the man he was supposed to be in your life. As time went on you became married and tried to build an empire for the family. God knows, you didn't know what he had in store for you. You have five children that you loved so dearly, three of your own and your two bonus children God allowed you to have, which has been blessings to you.

Being in a marriage has been the toughest task you had to work on in your life. Learning that it's just not about you anymore, but it's about "us" now. You had your share of ups and downs, but there was this one situation that you had to deal with due to infidelity in your marriage. The question that you asked yourself was, "should I go, or should I stay?" That's when you noticed growth in your spiritual life. Through the hurt and pain, you recognized that the love of your life was being attacked spiritually. The level of trust you had, wasn't there anymore. As you push past the pain, you told yourself, "I'm not giving up, this will work, I will save my marriage," and you did. What you did was forgive the love of your life, second you called the other person that was involved and forgive them for what they had done, so that you can move on with your life. You have a happy family and you will not let anyone tear you apart. You learned the art of cutting off the enemies'

head right when it rises.

Sincerely,
Your Spiritual Warrior

Psalm from a Spiritual Warrior

God, I thank you for giving me a heart that is willing to forgive, even when the pain is unbearable, you still want us to forgive and move on. Thank you for the family you have given to me, thank you for the love we have for each other, and ultimately the love we have for you will keep us for an eternity. Thank you, God.

Diary 12
The Emancipation of "Ressey"
Co-Author Carese Gayle

Letter 1: Don't plant your feet in the space between the Stones

Never neglect the stones in your life that are solid enough to uphold you by wasting time with the spaces between the stones
-Angela N. Brand

Dear Ressey

You learned a valuable lesson today; "Don't plant your feet in the space between the stones." Those were Aunt Claire's exact words. Do you remember what you did instead? The funeral took up the whole day. You pretended to read along in the hymn books and played with the frilly socks your aunt put you in every Sunday. The tropical heat was unbearable, but you could hear the rain tapping on the tin roof top and knew as soon as they let you out of there you were going to find the biggest puddle you could to splash in. The excitement shot through your small body causing you to squirm around in your seat. Auntie glanced down at you through her large frame glasses, and you became a statue. The pastor instructed everyone to come to the front and view the body. You didn't even know who died, or what it even meant to die. Your aunt stopped you on the way to the front.

The rain intensified as you left the church. The choir sang even more passionately, determined not to be drowned out by the rain. "Yet sings my soul our savior unto thee, how great thou art, how great though art." Steam started to rise from the crowd of people and each drop of rain took away all the stresses of the day and filled your body with delight. Your aunt and you walked out to the large stone field with the rectangle walk way. You walked single filed across the church yard jumping from stone to stone unknowing what lied beneath your feet until you reached the large empty hole in the ground. Each person standing on a grey stone block crying, singing, and praising. You, sliding, splashing, and jumping. Aunt Claire glanced down at you and uttered the words "Don't plant your feet in the space between the stones." You smiled and continued your bliss. You twirled and watched with awe as your dress ballooned around you and collapsed with dizziness...

Then you saw it. Lodged in the middle of the stones. It had a pretty pink flower attached to it, but it was the picture of the woman in the photo that caught your attention. It was your friend Miss V, you couldn't wait to collect the picture, so you could bring it home and show her that the church had pictures of her. You imagine she would scuff and complain about her hair or hang it up in her room if she thought it was one of her better ones. Either way she had to know. Miss V had come to help take care of you and your elderly auntie about a year ago. She cooked and cleaned and always found time to play with you. The last time you showed her the crickets you found in the back yard she shrieked and ran full speed to her room. You giggled and tried to force them under her door.

You stretched out into the puddle of water to rescue the photo. But it seemed as if something was holding it down. You glanced over at Auntie, she was in a deep embrace with a church sister. The picture had begun to float away so you placed your leg in the side of the stone and the other in between. All at once your tiny body disappears into a murky grave puddle. You tried to scream but they turn into gurgles of muddy water bubbles. You kick but there is no end or begging no bottom or top. You gasp for air inhaling nothing but the swampy water. Somehow you can still hear the sound of the choir singing. "Yet sing my soul. My savior unto thee, how great though art. How great though art." Your Auntie Claire was the first person you saw when that sunlight hit your face. She was crying even more than before and embraced you as if she never planned to let you go. The entire congregation cheered and prayed over your rescue. Best of all you had rescued the photo. Despite the day you had, you were still filled with glee. You would show Miss V the picture you found of her earlier and even more about the huge puddle you found.

Knock, knock" no answer "KNOCK, KNOCK" Nothing. You lie on the ground and peek under her door. "Miss V, guess what I found at church today"

Can I come in?" "Miss V?" You slide the picture under her door and wait.

AUNTIE!"

Normally Miss V would have put on her creepiest voice and scratched at the door to scare you off. She would sing at the top of her lungs and pretend not to hear you. She would at least sneak around the house and appear right behind you with a pot and spoon in hand to knock on. But, there was only silent, no jokes, no laughter.

She was gone, you finally realize why auntie Claire was crying, and why Miss V's face was on the picture, we were at her funeral, and now you had a better understanding of the whole day; now you understand why you knocked on her door and there was no answer, why that room was silent, why the house seems to be engulf in grief; it made you sad to know she left without saying good bye.

As I think back, now I am realizing the message; you don't even think Aunt Claire even knew what that message was. But today it is clear, I've spent the past few years neglecting the people I love. Always believing they are only a phone call away. Focusing my energy on people who can come into my life one day and leave the next. These people are my rocks; my stones if you will. I have planted my feet in the wrong places. In the space between the stones. On unstable ground. The memory of Miss V has reignited that message "Don't plant your fee in the space between the stones" and I thank the Lord for this revelation and now I can go from stone to stone.

Psalm to the Lord

Dear God,

God, thank you for giving me the revelation to stop wasting valuable time between the spaces, sinking in relationships that could not uphold me. I thank you for everything Miss V has taught me and the memories I still have of her. You have been there every step of the way, guiding and keeping me from dangers seen and unseen, you are a good God to me, I am truly grateful.

In Jesus name

Amen

Letter 2: It's Not Fair

*Some things in life we go through are not fair, but those things come to shape
and mold us into the people we are supposed to be.*

Dear Carese,

You're right, "*It's Not Fair*": only white girls get good dads. The world
tells you so. I see that envy in your eyes when you watch those little
white girls across the street, snuggle up in their father's lap. I can tell
you wish you could climb up right beside them and hold him tight and
feel protected. You imaged he'd smell like aftershave just like the dads
on TV. When your father comes to live with you, you image he will scare
off all the knuckle-head boys who tried to date you. Only the best for hi
baby girl. And once a suitable man can impress him, he will walk you
down the aisle with tears in his eyes beaming with pride. Your dad will
show you how to ride a bike and teach you to drive. He will come to all
your softball games and tell you to steal second base. He will call you
his princess, because that is what daddy suppose to call his little girl,
right? So that's what you will be, his perfect little princess.

You tortured your mom with endless questions about how they
met and when he would come and stay with you. You pushed and
prayed, and when the day finally came you wore your prettiest pink
dress and really got your elbows good with the Vaseline. Your mom
chuckled at the sight of your oily face and Sunday's best outfit. You met

him once before, when you visited Jamaica. It was the day the two of you walked more than 5 miles to meet your aunts and uncles. You struggled to keep up, but he'd never know it. You would hop and leap and take 3 steps to his one. He was impressed with your stamina, you could tell. He would ask you if you were tired or need to stop but breaks were for suckers and your daddy's daughter was no sucker. He was dreamy, tall, dark and handsome. His skin was like lavender, in color and texture. His smile was contagious. He would glance down at you and flash his beautiful smile and you couldn't help but to return the favor. He wore a colorful fishnet tank top like most island men did and smoked his Matarhan brand cigarette the entire way. It didn't bother you though. You told him you were used to the smell when he asked. He chuckled at the obvious lie. In that moment he was your dad and everything you dreamed he would be. You were so proud to have him and know him and be able to call him your own.

The moment finally came, daddy was home at last, but "It's Not Fair", he is not what I thought he would be, "It's Not Fair" that a little girl must deal with this from her father. Now, you were torn in this moment, you needed to make a choice. You can tell your mother about his betrayal or you can hold on to the hope that he will change. The same hope I'm sure your mom is clinging to. He's already threatened you with the withdrawal of his love if you say a word. When that woman put that child in your arms and told you he was your brother, you glanced at you father for guidance with no clue how to react. He continued to smoke his cigarette and gave you a nod and kept his eyes locked on you. You looked back at the baby boy, he was cute, and his smile was just like your dad, contagious. You had to fight back the urge; he was dressed impeccably wearing a Coogie sweater and a pair of Jordan sneakers. You glanced at your own feet and instantly became compelled to hand him back. Before you could, Breanna, your 5-year-old sister broke the silence squealing "Hi brother" with playful glee. She began to dance and kiss the infant and everyone marveled at the overwhelming cuteness.

So, you just sat still; frozen between the legs of this woman's who you knew was sleeping with your father behind you mothers back, her son on your lap fresher than you. Each braid took an eternity, but what other option did you have. When you got home your mother marveled over the braids and how well done they were. It made you cringe when your dad chimed in with praise of his mistresses braiding skills. When you eventually escaped to your room you battled with the decision you had to make. Why should you be his protector? It's Not Fair! He was never there to protect you. Was he protecting you when he had you trafficking drugs at 12 years old? It's Not Fair! What about when he stomped you like a man with his size 12 timberline's after coming home late from softball practice. It's Not Fair! You had to use half a bottle of your mom's concealer to cover all the scars. The mental ones remain. It's Not Fair! What about when he kissed your lips while wrestling playfully and quickly realized his error. To cover up his slip, he decided to spit in your mouth and tossed you across the room like a rag doll. It's Not Fair!

Even your poor baby sister endured his torment. She inherited that deep melanated skin from him. You had to guard her from his anger countless times. His disdain for her reflected his own insecurity. Not even one "I love you." No proud Papa moments. The one time he tried to teach you to drive he shook your nerves so bad you put off the milestone much longer than you should have. Think of the pain your mother, endured. You hear her sobbing from the distance. It's no longer abnormal to you. Some nights she spends hours in the mirror making sure every hair is in place slipping into her prettiest dress and paints her face to perfection. All to watch her excitement diminish and her makeup slowly melt off her face with each tear. He even has the gall to sweet talk these women on the phone right in front of you. Illiterate ass, YOU had to pronounce half their names for his ass before he could even call. It was repulsive, he would lean all the way back, feet up, a hand down his pants, all cozy and shit in your mom's house, on HER couch, on HER phone. It's Just Not Fair!

Girl, think of the time he picked you up from school. All the girls wooned over him. It made you proud for a moment. That is until one of them bellowed out "Aye that's my weed man." They clowned you for weeks. Do you remember your uncle running up those stairs bat in hand and fire in his eyes after hearing him bark at his sister so loud, he wouldn't be a man if he didn't intervene? You can end it right now, no more fighting, no more tears, no more midnight visits from the police. This is your chance Carese; so, what if he "disowns" you. He's doesn't deserve your loyalty. I see you studying your baby brother's portrait.

Light caramel completion, deep brown eyes, and of course sporting your daddy's smile. All you can think is; He doesn't even care. He allowed his mistress to give you evidence of his infidelity. I already know how it ends. I'm sure you're curious to know. Although you prayed nightly for God to remove him from your life, even after the constant arrest and daily mental abuse you endured. You still love him. He is your dad and you are proud to have him and know him and call him your own. But It's still Not Fair, even after all he put us through, you still have love for him, it not fair.

Prayer of Reese

Dear God,

Grant me a forgiving heart, to allow my earthly father back into my life, give me the patience to receive and accept his flaws and the man that he is with an open mind and heart. Thank you in advance.

In Jesus name,

Amen

Letter 3: YOU are the Prize

Never give your prize to those who are not willing to pay the price
-Angela N. Brand

Dear Prize

Imagine a day when he offers you everything. The ring, the house, the family, *Everything.* Can you imagine turning it all down? Well, that's exactly how it happened. Almost 6 years had passed since the day you left Connecticut. When you moved or as he put it "ran away" to North Carolina, you started your career, focused on health and wellness wore your hair natural. All the things you wanted to do. You even dated other men. Yes girl, there are *OTHER men.* Through each new experience you evolved and realized your worth.

It came in the form of an email. The subject read, *"I Should have never let you go."* Your eyes were fixed on the words, imagining the contents. Could this be real? When you made your decision to leave he took vengeance on you, prepared to draw blood. He sent you countless pictures of his many conquests. Destroyed everything you worked for. Moved that woman into your home. Rubbed your face in his new relationships. Revealed all the intimate secrets of your time together. Destroyed your character and reputation. You weren't so sure you even wanted to read it. Nevertheless, you clicked. Here's what it said:

Dear Ressey,

hope this letter finds you. I realized you blocked me from all areas of
our life. But I've got to try. I've thought of you every day since you left.
arese, you were perfect in every way. I look back at the man I was
ack then, I know now that I wasn't a man at all. I was a little boy, not
eady for this gift that God had blessed me with. It was never you
essey, it was always me. I'm the reason we didn't work out. I sabotaged
ur relationship because I was afraid. I knew I couldn't be the man you
eeded me to be. I didn't want you to see me for what I really was, lost
nd immature. I knew you were special, so I convince you that I was the
rize when all along it was you. Where will I find another Carese? I
ate that it's taken me so long to come to this revelation. You probably
ate me, I would hate me too. I want you to know that I never stopped
oving you. My love for you is more than I can put in words. Please give
ie the chance to see you again. I have some things going on in
harlotte and I can pretend like that's the reason for wanting so badly
o come there. But the reality is, I want more than anything else to see
our face again, and hear your voice, and see you smile. Please give me
iis last chance."

You sat motionless before your computer screen. Here he was
ouring his heart out to you. The only man you had ever loved. No
assing blame or trying to minimize his trespasses. A complete apology
or every bit of hurt he caused you. And what did you feel? Nothing! No
verwhelming joy, no excitement, no tears. You were 18 when you met
im. Now at 28 you're not even sure if you're the same person he's

writing to. But at that moment, you know the one you are imagining right now. That moment had been playing in the back of your mind since the day you packed you bags and left. You had to go.

The drive to the restaurant was silent. No radio. Just the sound of the road and your thoughts. Your 5 years together was a whirlpool of deception. He had taken an innocent naïve girl and broke her spirit. You thought of the time he maxed out your very first credit card before you even took the first swipe. The time he locked you out of your home in the cold Connecticut winter just to spite you. You're still convinced he took your car and sold it for profit. You saved for a whole year for that car and never even drove it. Not to mention the child, you know about, the one he had with his ex- WIFE while you were together. Yes, she was his wife. And of course, you can't forget the countless women of which he himself provided proof. There were good times sandwiched in there. The late-night studio sessions where you bonded over your love of music, the weekend getaways and luxury vacations. And the bond you forged with his family and friends was incredible. But, that was all in the past.

You arrived at the restaurant hair pulled back in a sleek bun. Red silk blouse and black pencil skirt. Yes, girl you know we Slayed. The room paused when you walked in. All eyes were on you. You scanned the room twice over, but no sign of him. Suddenly you hear a familiar voice calling from behind. "Ressey" it had been so long since anyone called you Ressey, it sound so sweet you wondered why you ever retired that nickname. You spun around and locked eyes with him. His

240

smile was as bright as the North Star. Same chocolate skin and squinty little eyes you had grown to love. He was smaller than you remembered. He stood about 5'10" but you still towered over him in your heels. His wrist was laced with gold and platinum jewelry, chains, bracelets and watches. He wore an oversized button-down shirt and his pants had manmade rips and tears. Not quite the type you had grown to be attracted to. You gave each other a deep embrace and examined one another for a moment. There he was standing right in front of you after all this time; and what you thought you would feel; you didn't. You had dinner and drinks and loosed up a bit. You laughed and reminisced and even made fun of some of your silly antics from back in the day. But it wasn't the same.

He was expecting Ressey, the fun and vulnerable young girl with little life experience. Instead he met Carese, the conscious woman with a direction and standard for her life. At the end of the night, he asked you. "Why don't we try this again? I'm not the same man I was back then. I will never treat you less than you deserve again. I want to start a family with you and grow old together. I'm looking into buying a house here and opening a few studios. I just don't want to lose you again Ressey." You paused, not knowing what to say. Noticing your hesitation, he continued. "I mean, you can think about it. You don't have to make your decision now. I know this is a lot and I'd hate for you to make a rush decision. I love you. I just want another chance to see if this could work." You reached for your glass of Merlot and took a slow till sip. "I can't" that was it. That's all you said. He waited for more, preparing his response. "I just can't do it, it was great to see you again and catch up. I wish you the best in all that you do, but my life has taken a different direction. I want you to know that I forgive you for everything but I'm not willing to go backwards" It was hard for you to see his face drop and his eyes pool over with tears. But, your feelings had changed. He was no longer the apple of your eye. The sun and moon were no longer directed by him. You had grown so much from the person you are today. You left that restaurant that day knowing that if you had the courage to turn down the one constant in your life, you had the courage to accomplish all your dreams.

So, go ahead, call your mom, she will get you through this. When she comes, she will hold your hand the entire way. She will reassure you that you're making the right decision. Get up off that floor; you will not be a doormat forever. And remember, it was never you. You are the Prize, you've always been.

Prayer from the Prize

Dear God,

Thank you for giving me the clarity to recognize when something or someone is not good for me, and for giving me the courage to assert my independence and to evolve into the woman I am today.

In Jesus name,

Amen

Letter 4: True Beauty

True beauty is never on the outside, it is the reflection of one's soul.
-Angela N. Brand

Dear Beauty

Yes, baby girl, she is *BEAUTIFUL*. You will be a beauty as well. Yes, her *GRACE* is unmatched. You will have a grace of your own. Yes, her *STYLE* is unparalleled. Yours will be unique to you. Yes, her *DRIVE* is unimaginable. You will push yourself so hard you will break walls. I know right now it seems impossible. All women have their battles, even her. There will come a day when you will step into a room and your light will illuminate your presence. Your *COLOR* will develop into its full rich tone. Your *HAIR* will strengthen to a tight and deliberate curl, and your *EYES* will deepen with the wisdom and clarity of a life well earned. And Yes, at times you're going to feel out of place when compared to the beauty standards of the future, but you can't compare where you don't compete, and baby girl you don't have to. You must value your royal roots but that doesn't mean everyone else will. I wish I could tell you that this is where it ends, but no. Throughout your life outsiders will continually attempt to demean your greatness to mask their own insecurities. You must understand that YOU ARE PERFECT, YOU ARE GREAT, YOU ARE MAGNIFICENT, just the way you are.

Prayer of Thanksgiving

Thank you, God, for allowing me to see the beautiful person you created me to be; you know God that for a while I did not believe the narrative that I saw reflected in the mirror; I could not see it because I was too busy believing what I was told by others. Now I have the confidence to see the true beauty that lies on the inside and outside of me, thank you for showing that to me.

In Jesus name,

Amen

Letter 5: Way to Grow

True maturity is measured by one's ability to grow.
-Angela N. Brand

Dear Future Carese,

You've been on my mind lately. I've been fixed on the present and spent very little time putting you first. I want you to know that you are the most important person in my world.

Take these vows as a token of my devotion to you:

- I vow to end our love hate relationship. I will no longer inflict doubt and insecurities on you.
- I vow to have faith in my intuition and know that where ever it guides me is exactly where I'm meant to be.
- I vow to find my purpose. I will show passion in everything I do in order to feel whole from within.
- I vow to never abandon my character. I will remain kind yet fortified. I will not allow myself to be influence by the world around me.
- I vow to require the same love I have for myself from my partner. I will never settle for less than what I know I deserve.
- I vow to have a vision and a purpose for my future, so that I won't return to the familiar that is in my past.
- I vow to spend more time with my family. I will focus more on the people I love and those who love me.
- I vow to take care of you inside and out. Mine, body, and soul and spirit

- I wow not to seek validation from those who are not qualified to provide it.
- I vow to love you, so that when true love beckons, you will recognize it and it won't seem like an unfamiliar event.
- I vow to make myself accountable for my actions and (Take Ownership) for every decision.
- I vow to give back to my community. I will do all I can to uplift the next generation.
- I vow to find value from within, so that no one will ever be able devalue you.
- I vow to be my authentic self, not a false representation of what I think others want me to be.
- I vow to represent you better than I have in the past. I will live on purpose with a design and direction to my life.

Now, I'm going to do my part, here's what I need from you.

If you're lucky enough to still have her, call your mom.

Never stop improving in case you forgot this along the way.

Don't worry so much about aging, youth has no age and your spirit is forever young. Knowing that each experience has molded you into the woman you are today.

Most important, don't have any regrets you've made all the right decisions, and remember I've got your back. Life is tough but so are you, and you know how to make your dreams come through.

Prayer from the Grower

Dear God,

Give me the strength to uphold these vows and to live a purpose driven life, please continue to cover me with your love, allow me to continue to trust your work, and to know that you have already planned and designed my future, beyond my wildest dreams.

In Jesus name,

Amen

I Stand as You

stand as the woman who wants to give up and throw in the towel who hought to herself, going through all this is definitely not worth the ight.

The woman, who had all odds against her and can't bear it all.

The woman who took those pills because the pressure from the pain vas just too damn hard.

Stand as You

The woman, who was molested at the tender age of 5-years old, vondering how to move past the pain.

The woman, who sold her body and danced for the dollar, who is shamed to hold her head up high.

Stand as You

The woman, who took the black eyes and was beaten for no apparent eason, wondering, praying, hoping wishing, Lord just get me out of this raziness.

The woman who devalued her body and lost her identity all because of he words "I love you".

ee Beautiful Soul I Stand as You

he woman who fought for her life through trials and tribulations, just o get ahead

he woman who fasted and prayed just to get breakthrough, wondering iod where are you?

stand as the woman who took the blows of life, fail on her face, but bund the strength to get back up again

The woman who was walked out on, gave up on, spit on, lied on, cheated on, and stabbed in the back by the people who claim to love her.

I Stand as You

When I stand, I stand as the 10,000 women who walk in shame and embarrassment of her past; when people said her you will never be nothing.

When I stand, I stand as the woman who couldn't stand for herself, when all odds were against her.

I Stand as You

The woman who stand in the mirror piecing herself apart looking for flaws that are just not there, comparing herself to other women not knowing their struggle.

The woman who had broken fragments of her imagination torn into pieces, wondering, if her dream will ever come true.

I Stand as You

The woman who decided that living a common life was no longer an option, but striving to be my best version of herself, "At All Cost"

I Stand as You

The woman who decided strength is my new wardrobe, integrity is my new hat, and power is my new pair of shoes.

I Stand as You

The woman who realized her Mess became her Message and not ashamed to own her truth, knowing it will set others free

Stand as You

The woman who started that business knowing all odds were against her believing she was great and had something to offer the world

The woman who had the life changing moment knowing the Power of Endurance would see her through

Stand as You

also stand for the 1Million female business owners who had to fight their way up to the top knowing welfare used to be her source, oh but now, she is the trailblazer setting paths for other women to follow.

Stand as You

The woman who was hated on because she received a coat of many colors, battle snakes at night and demons that tormented her mind

Stand as You

The woman who sold all she had, just to get her purse right

The woman who is Flexin in her complexion, knowing she looks good in her brown skin.

Stand as You

stand as the woman who battled with forgiving herself and felt she wasn't good enough to be great.

The woman who had her dreams shattered and searching for love in all the wrong places

Oh! Yeah Queen, I Stand as You

The woman who was birthed into her Queendom and received a kingdom with all access granted.

The woman who acknowledge the Errors of her Life and became the Transformed Survivor.

I Stand as You

The woman who Took Ownership of Who she Was, Where she Was, Where she has Been and Where she is Going.

The Woman who was dealt an unfair hand in life but bounced back with pride and dignity.

I Stand as You

"

The woman who was a Warrior Princess learned to fight in the spirit to possess the promises of God.

The woman whose dreams were set on high and Raised from the Ashes

I Stand as You

The woman who shares her Queendom Diaries all to live the Queendom Life.

See I believe when real Queens stand they stand to be Bold but Beautiful, Courageous but Calm, Fierce but Feminine.

I Stand as You, will you Stand as "Me Too"

This poem was inspired by Maya Angelou and Oprah Winfrey
-Angela N. Brand

Conclusion

Now, you are already at the end. We hope you've enjoyed reading our diaries, and pray you were inspired, motivated and felt our compassion, as we took the time to share our diaries with you; please take the time to post on our social media platforms of how this book blessed you. Please encourage everyone you know to get a copy of this book. Our goal is to empower the world with stories of our truth as it relates to our life struggles, trials, and disappointments.

You may find yourself in one or more of the situations we shared with you; don't stay isolated in fear, rejection and shame of what you have been through. Reach out to us and make a lifetime connection with women who care about you and your freedom to be yourself, and how God created you.

References

Nelson's NKJV Study Bible, formally titled The Nelson Study Bible NKJV 1997. Thomas Nelson Inc.

Hughes, Langston, 1902-1967. The Collected Poems of Langston Hughes. New York :Knopf : Distributed by Random House, 1994. Print.

AB ENTERPRISE INC.

You maybe to saying yourself, this book touched my soul and I must be a part of The Queendom Diaries series or I have a story I want to tell that will touch the hearts of people, like this book touched my heart. Or there is a training book, workbook manual or any other writings I would like to do. If you said yes that's "me", AB Enterprise Inc. is here or your publishing needs, to get your manuscript out to the world. Allow AB Enterprise Inc. to help you be seen, get heard and Branded by writing your book with us. www.queendomlifeuniversity.com

The QUEENDOM DIARIES
"pages from the diary of a queen"
The Book & Coaching Workbook

Audio Book Coming Soon!
www.queendomlifeuniversity.com amazon

Embrace your Inner Child and Set Her FREE!

To take full advantage of Healing the Inner Child, this workbook is available for you through Amazon or www.queendomlifeuniversity.com Allow this coaching journal to guide you in the process to wholeness. You will learn and be coached on the 8 Dimensions of Embracing your Inner Child that will allow you to live a victorious adult life to the fullest. If you need or desire life coaching, please reach out to one of the authors you most feel connected to and see how she can transform your life by helping you Embrace your Inner Child. Don't sit in silent sufferings, asking the question, "When will I be free from this?"

Allow one of us to help you. Take Action Now!

AB Life Coaching Certification

"Training for the 21st Century Coach"

n this 8-week training certification program, individuals looking to start or continue this training in coaching learn essential tools to start or advance their coaching business. During this class you will learn powerful techniques of coaching that will transform your life and the life of your clients. You will learn how to development profitable programs and services, how to market and brand yourself as a professional coach.

You may be asking yourself how will if I know I'll make a good life coach? If you answer yes to any of the questions below, then you will make a great coach:

1. Do you love people?
2. Do people come to you for advice or with their problems?
3. Do you desire to see others win?
4. Do you have a heart for people or a desire to see them healed and set free?
5. Are you creative in thinking of great services and events?
6. Do you speak with power and passion when talking about your purpose?
7. Do you always have answers to problems?
8. Are you good in coming up with strategies?
9. Are you a solution driven person?
10. Do you see the good in everyone?

For further details please visit:
https://www.queendomlifeuniversity.com/ablifecoachingcertification

Speaking w/ Power & Passion
Coaching & Training for Motivational Speakers

Do you want to make a GREATER IMPACT while speaking?
-and book more engagements?

Are you ready to take you speaking career to the next level or you are just starting and need training to become a one of a kind speaker.? Do you want to learn how to engage your audience and get them to take action?

      Speaking w/ Power and Passion is an 8 week coaching program for speakers to improve their speaking skills. During the coaching session you will learn what type of speaker you are, the purpose and the mindset of a speaker.

As a Result of coaching with AB, you will have

1. Confidence when selling
2. Clarity of who you are as a speaker
3. How to SHOW-UP Powerfully
4. Power in delivering your speech
5. Passion when telling your story
6. Techniques of Selling
7. Insight of how to engage your audience
8. Crafting your Signature Closing

For more details please visit
https://www.queendomlifeuniversity.com/speaking-w-power-and-passion

About the Authors

Angela N. Brand, is a Best-Selling Author, Publisher, Master Trainer, Certified Life Coach, Powerful Empowerment and Motivational Speaker Inspiring individuals all over the world to "Take Ownership" of Who they Are, Where they Are, Where they Been, and Where they are Going. She is the Founder/CEO of AB Enterprise which Queendom Life University is an entity, where she trains coaches and speakers to get paid to be themselves through the AB Life Coaching & Speaking w/ Power & Passion Certification Programs. AB believes because of her struggle of rejection and self-identity crisis, being molested multiple times by 6 different men from the tender age of 5 to 19 years old, she was called to empower women to discover their true purpose in life by embracing their Mess as their Message. Her mission is to make an impact in the world through her message and motivate people to grow and reach for their highest potential.

AB received the 2017 Phenomenal Women Trailblazer Award from the Black Heritage Association. She has been trained by one the world greatest motivational speakers Lisa Nichols's" Speak for Ultimate Impact and Profit" and "The Speak and Write to make Millions" workshops. AB have read, studied and listened to over 1,000 videos and books in her field, believing all great leaders continue learning as a tool of advancements and have superb mentors and coaches that will push them to their greatness.

She has also been featured as a Co-Hostess on "Ladies on Assignment Talk Show" found on The Word Network, Preach the Word Network, YouTube and FaceBook. AB has a radio show called "Queendom Life Radio" found on WDRB Media, inspiring woman all over the globe through her message of hope and faith. Coach AB is also the Life Coach of Gracious Hands Transitional Housing helping women to create goals, overcome obstacles and break repeated cycles in their life.

The Power House Speaker knows how to get audiences engaged and inspired to take action, taking you places within yourself that you did not know you can go. While serving beyond the call of duty she will provoke the champion within you to arise and step into the ring of life. Although AB has many accomplishments, she has the heart of a servant and is fueled with passion to see others reach the unreachable and obtain what was once unattainable in their life.

Contact Coach AB

Email:
www.queendomlifeuniversity.com
FaceBook:
    @TheQueendomCoachAB
    @QueendomLifeRadio
    @QueendomDiaries
IG: TheQueendomCoach
TW: QueendomCoach

Turkessia J. Barnes was born in 1990, in Atlanta, GA to Billy and Elizabeth Johnson, and raised in Stone Mountain, GA, where she completed all her schooling from Elementary to High School. In 2008, she graduated from Stone Mountain High School. Shortly afterwards, she started college, she decided to give herself a fresh start and go after something she felt she wanted. So in 2009, she entered the Georgia Piedmont Technical College of Cosmetology, she quickly realized this program was not going to be available as she thought, overwhelmed by the thought of not moving forward, she knew she had to make a choice, so she decided to take a few business classes until the class she really wanted became available; she fell in love with all the knowledge she gained, so she stayed with Business. In 2011, she gave birth to her daughter London Helen Okeh, and in 2013, she later gave birth to her second daughter Leslie Amarachi Okeh.

She was a single mom determined to make a difference. After giving birth to her daughter Leslie, a shift happened; she began to be more aware of herself and the community she lived in. She knew there was more God had for her, so she joined a local church, re-dedicated her life to Christ, left an almost 5 years, emotionally abusive relationship, became celibate, and spent a lot of time with God. At this time, God began to deal with the matters of her heart. He accelerated her to make a difference and quickly placed her on assignment. In the same year, she founded Lambs & Hearts Ministries, which is now, Evolution Ministries, and began feeding the homeless of Atlanta, GA. This ministry serves over 250 people per month from a food truck. She later partnered with churches in her community to assist in small prayer groups as she passed out meals. During this time, she witnessed many women and children being stranded on the streets, and they had the most horrific stories of things that happened to them during this time, she spent many nights toiling, praying and even crying after her monthly feed.

After much prayer, she knew she had to do more: she became bold, and started housing single mothers and their children in her home, one family at a time. In April 2014, she organized and hosted Vision Board Parties to encourage single and married mothers to set clear goals and created a "Mini Success Guide," based on her knowledge, to assist in that process. She then partnered with local community centers, creating programs for single mothers as herself, pushing them to stay on their goals, get assistance, apply for jobs and not end up on the streets. For the past five years she has been active in her community, serving on several councils and representing the women in her community.

She was awarded by her community for her service to the many families she supports. She continues to create innovative programs for mothers and their children by motivating many young mothers to home school their children. And encourage the process and procedures of *Parents as Teachers*, as well as approved many activities to support family engagement.

During this time, she pushed herself, determined, she went on to complete two degrees, in Business Management (2013) & Human Resource Management (2017) from Georgia Piedmont Technical

College, and earned several certificates in Business and Administration, all as a single mother.

While she is still active in her community, her greatest accomplishment is being a great example for her children London (7) and Leslie (4). London is the Founder of London Kelechi Helen Okeh Productions, and is the author of "Pretty Girl, Pretty Girl Princess" and Leslie is the Founder of "Little Miss Sassy," and has published her first book as well. Her children are both ambassadors of GirlPreneur Academy, a business spearheaded by Turkessia, which was inspired by them to help young girls know they can to have their own businesses at any age, doing what they love. Turkessia recently became engaged to McKinley Hodges, Jr. and is Co-Author of this amazing book anthology of healing.

Turkessia currently has set her mind on transforming lives through her organizations to make a greater impact on people's, she works heavily in church and has branded herself to reach greater platforms to produce greater help. She desires to be the face of change for her community, which pushed her into her next steps for school, as she will be majoring in Social Work and Divinity. She is also working on her first book, "The Birthing of a Queen" and her first E- book, The Language of Prayer". She is a firm believer of Christ and his ability to make any situation successful. She is not ashamed of who she is, what she has, and where she is going. She has a passion for helping others to push past their circumstances to make Christ the head of their lives, so they too can see how God can change them for the better.

Courtney Smith is a native of Columbus, GA. the daughter of the late Rev. Ronald Smith and Pamela Smith (living) and a mother of three. She is a graduate of Troy University where she obtained her bachelor's degree in Psychology and a minor in Human Services. In addition, Smith is an Inspirational/Motivational Speaker, Life coach, author, and Vlogger (Courtney Smith #selflove/YouTube). Above all, Courtney is God's child who discovered a new life through him by first learning to love me first.

Her purpose and passion is to help women heal from their broken places in life so they can become the total woman God created them to be, so they like herself can live a life authentically and unapologetically. Taking her personal struggles with depression, anxiety, low self-esteem, and self-worth she decided she wanted a new life and no longer just exist so, that forced her to put in the work to live by shifting the hurt to healing, pain to power, and now visions to reality These letters and prayers are for you. God Bless

#SELFLOVE

Georgia Gayle is originally from Jamaica West Indies, she migrated to the States almost 30 years ago and has lived in New Haven CT for most of those years, and she is the mother of three daughters. She relocated to Charlotte NC in 2007. Georgia holds a master's Degree in Adult Education and Training, a bachelor's Degree in business administration, and is two classes away from a master's Degree in Business, i.e. {MBA} with a concentration in Marketing. She also obtained her Life Coach certification in February of 2018.

Georgia is also a Women' Empowerment speaker; she has been invited to speak several times here in Charlotte, as well as Atlanta, GA and Dallas TX; her goal is to transform women in becoming better version of themselves. Georgia also serves as the Business Coach, for Queendom Life University.

Georgia has been a volunteer teacher in the Mecklenburg school system through a program called Citizen School since 2014, where she taught Business classes to middle school students. She has worked in the Banking and Insurance field for more than 15 years and is currently working in the Cable industry for more than five years, where she has received several awards as a top agent.

Mary J. Wade (Cantrell) was born and raised in Knoxville, TN, the youngest of five children. Mary was a quick study and fast learner, often being found in the local library. It was the place that she could travel the world without leaving home. She graduated from Austin-East High school, the Valedictorian of her class, and fondly recalls participating in many activities, to include band (where she was Drum Major and played several instruments), track/field and ROTC. Mary attended Tennessee State University and received a B.S. in Mechanical Engineering. At TSU she was also part of the Tigerbelle track team under the direction of Olympic legend the late Coach Ed Temple. She immediately began her career at Ford Motor Co. and has worked for major companies including TVA, Lockheed Aeronautical, and General Electric, of which she currently has 20-years tenure with expertise in Power Generation. There she mentors young people in STEM careers. Mary is an Engineer, Life Coach, Speaker, Author, Singer and Entrepreneur. She notes her greatest accomplishment is surviving some detrimental hardships on her journey and seeing her children thrive in of spite.

Mary is married to Maurice D. Wade Sr., residing in the greater Atlanta area. As a blended family they are the parents of 7 young adults. Their mission is to be an example of marriage success to their children and other blended families.

www.maryjwade.com

Sylvia Blue is the CEO/Owner of Prosperous Enterprise LLC. She has extensive experience in the Finance Industry, with private industry and non-profit organizations. Sylvia provides quality services and support to a diverse customer base by assessing customers' needs and satisfying customer expectations. Her business and personal credit restoration and credit protection plan members have documented results expanding their businesses and purchasing their dream homes.

Ms. Blue is also the CEO/President of A Sister's Heart, Inc., a faith-based non-profit organization, which provides resources, workshops and encouragement to abused/impoverished women in Wilson/Nash counties in North Carolina and Atlanta, Georgia. This organization was established to help the children of God by bringing about a healing and deliverance in their life from abuse and for them to obtain a life of wholeness.

Sylvia encourages her clients and those struggling with economic disparity with her life's motto: *"Your faith in His word has to be stronger than what you see! Don't let appearances take you out the game!"*

She is a Trustee of Higher Elevation International Ministries, in Douglasville, Georgia, the Blessed mother of three sons and one daughter, grandmother of two grandsons, a sister of seven siblings and an encourager of many.

Catherine Mitchell is a Certified Motivational Speaker through Queendom Life University under the Speaking w/Power & Passion speakers training. She has served in the Mental Health Community for 20 years and serves as an Assistant Behavior Therapist empowering children and adults to reach their highest potential regardless of their challenges in life.

C. Mitchell is the founder and CEO of F.A.R. Ministries where she works with women in building their confidence, self-worth and adds value to their lives. She is a Survivor of domestic violence of a 12-year relationship where she escaped the eye of death several times. Catherine's courageous attitude permitted her to be dedicated in the rescue and recovery of those still in bondage to their abuser. She now travels all over the world speaking and serving men and women to step into their greatness and live a life of freedom.

www.faraboverubies3.org
Cbmitchell76@gmail.com
www.CatherineMitchell.info

Spring C Jackson was born in California and grew up in the Chicago land area. Spring attended a Language Academy Magnet school on Chicago's North side where she learned the basics of the Italian language along with elementary studies. At thirteen years old she moved to Cedar Rapids, IA with family and attended high school. She currently resides in Cedar Rapids where she is working, pursuing her entrepreneurial endeavors and serves as a ministry leadership team member at Victorious Life Church.

Jackson has the enormous heart of a nurturer, mentor, and adult/child advocate solidifies her role as a Life Care Provider. She has been educated extensively in the areas of early childhood education and is a former small business owner. For six years she provided childcare as a registered in home childcare provider. Spring was a foster parent for four years and during that time, hosted a foreign exchange student from Kenya. She provides care for the intellectually delayed while currently pursuing a Bachelor's degree in Social Work.

Her personal experiences have cultivated her passion for children, which has developed into the implementation of her purpose. She is the founder and CEO of Abundant Life Care, a non-profit organization that gives children in the foster care system an alternative to institution or group care. Her organization will also be the host of her city's annual foster care conference as well as retreats for foster parents and workers. Please visit abundantlife.care for more information.

Spring is the owner of La Primavera, LLC. She is a Writer, Author Coach, Book Project Manager and Speaker. She wrote extensively as a child, including creative writings such as short stories and poetry but took a hiatus for years. Life just had to happen to give her more experiences in with which to talk about and she is finally ready to tell her stories of hardship, trouble and triumphs. Getting back into the writing process has not only given her own stories a voice but has given her the opportunity to realize her gift. Her ability to assist those in business with content writing and others with personal writing works, ensuring their ideas come alive through well-structured sentences and organized thought processes is immeasurable.

Min. Donna W. Figueroa is a Leadership and Career Coach; she is the CEO of Arete Government Services, which is in Arlington, VA. In her role, she uses her leadership skills and expertise in acquisition management and strategic planning to oversee the management of various programs as a consultant to the federal government. Donna is constantly sought out for acquisition resources and leadership management strategies. She has 19 years of federal service, to include Division Chief of the Department of State, Bureau Consular Affairs, General Services Division. Her leadership has resulted in the following policies and awards:

.. Coordinated the creation of an online Consular Supplies Status Folder, allowing Embassies/Consulates worldwide to check supply order status in real-time.

. Reorganized warehouse operations to ensure orders are received worldwide within 30-days of request.

. Franklin Meritorious Honor Cash Award & Medal for Exemplary Performance.

. Letter of Commendation- Passport Agency; Stamford, Connecticut; for implementation of acceptable administrative activities for the Purchase Card Program.

After many years of working in the federal government, she saw a need to fill the gap of leadership resources due to attrition and launched the Ignite Institute for Leaders and its subsidiary, the Ignite Institute for Women. Donna prepares future leaders by mentoring, resume building, the interview process, job placement and life skills development. She constantly gives back to her community. She is a licensed minister at the Greater Mount Calvary Holy Church in Washington, DC. She has also worked in the non-profit sector for over a decade; Donna provides leadership as the Director of Sandy Fork Community Corporation, a faith-based non-profit anti-poverty organization devoted to the impoverished residents of Wilson, Nash, and Edgecombe counties of North Carolina. Donna is a blessed wife, with a blended family, a mother of four and grandmother to ten.

Mrs. Figueroa was recently honored by The National Association of Professional Women (NAPW) as a 2017-2018 inductee into its VIP Woman of the Year Circle. She is recognized with this prestigious distinction for leadership in entrepreneurship. NAPW is the nation's leading networking organization exclusively for professional women, boasting more than 850,000 members, a thriving eChapter and over 200 operating Local Chapters. *I'm pleased to welcome Donna into this exceptional group of professional women,"* said *NAPW President Star Jones. "Her knowledge and experience in her industry are valuable assets to her company* and community."

With over 15 years' experience as an experienced Life Skills Coach and Facilitator, Donna is a sought after consultant, trainer, and aspiring author specializing in Organizational Leadership & Personal Development. Her expertise is in helping women identify, articulate, and execute their primary purpose. She coaches aspiring leaders to Ignite their leadership style up to the next level. "I believe that the journey to success both professionally and personally begins with mastering the relationship within one's self and others". Through reflective coaching practice her one-on-one and group facilitation sessions are leading scores of professionals and organizations into leading and living intentionally.

There's a Leader within – Ignite it!

Robin L. Johnson was reared in a single parent household by Ms. Sandra Johnson, in a close net community in the suburbs of Maryland. Robin discovered her calling and interest in helping the disadvantaged and disenfranchised at a young age. Sandra, who herself was displaced from her siblings by the death of her mother, was placed into the foster care system, but was blessed to be raised by Mr. and Mrs. George Jackson, a loving couple whom Robin recognizes as her devoted grandparents. This is where Robin undoubtedly developed her passion to help others. Her mother ironically became a foster parent, where Robin found herself helping to raise countless foster children.

Robin has been an asset to countless children ministries, youth ministries, and women ministries alike; she has served in the capacity of a Praise and Worship Leader, Youth empowerment Leader, Teacher, Prophetess, Minister and Elder. Aug 31, 2012, served as a milestone in Robin's life, when she was installed as Pastor of Created with Promise and Potential Ministries, which has since being renamed; Created to Win in 2017. Robin cherishes being a mother of four and grandmother for family is her first passion.

The second passion unmistakably is serving in ministry; either in singing gospel music, serving in the gospel the delivery of the gospel. In 1995, Robin co-founded Refuge Ministries, participated on countless boards, of which each established non- profit organization she held, targets the issues of the disadvantaged and disenfranchised. Robin understood the power of prayer and intercession, with that passion in June 2012; she cofounded Building Kingdom Walls Intercessors and ounded Fresh Fire Breakthrough Prayer Hour. Clearly, everyone that s acquainted with her knows women empowerment and sisterhood are at the top of her list as well; in 2012 she birthed of Woman to Woman mpartation (WTWI) ministry which hosts annual conference and empowering workshops.

In 2017 she launched Life Transitions with Coach Robin radio show, and Side Piece No More Chronicles women empowerment workshops. Pastor Robin also has a diverse multifaceted skill set from a teacher, author, event planner, workshop facilitator, motivational speaker along with pastoral services.

JaQuita J. Jackson born on November 20, 1986 (a native of Atlanta Georgia) reared by her grandparents; she was taught as a child how to develop a personal relationship with the Lord. She accepted Jesus Christ as her personal savior at the age of 17 and has persisted through her life challenges by celebrating her love for Jesus Christ in worship and praise. JaQuita was ordained a prophet and pastor in 2018 along with her husband Jeremy after accepting the call on their life to lead and help restore Gods people. They have three beautiful children Joshua, Janiya, and Justis.

This anointed prophet strongly believes in glorifying God in creative expression through Liturgical and Mime dancing as a form of praise and worship. She affirms that her dancing honors God, releases strongholds, and allows deliverance and healing to manifest her life, and in the lives of others.

JaQuita continues to pursue the call of God in her life by gaining a better understanding of the word of God. She has earned her bachelor's degree in Religious Studies at Beulah Heights University, and she completed her MBA at Ohio Christian University. Her goal in life is to continue to chase after God for her growth, empower others, and to give God glory!

She stands on,

"With God, all things are Possible. And I believe as long as I stay true to myself, continue to love my family, and remain humble, I'm good, because I know from whom my blessings come from.

Carese Gayle was born in the Caribbean Island of St. Catherine, Jamaica. She moved to the United States at the age of 5 with her mother to New Haven CT. She worked her way through the Banking industry and earned her way to the top sales agent for her region on several occasions. She later relocated to Charlotte NC and started her career in Insurance as an Agent, where she was promoted and recognized for her hard work and service. After many years in the insurance industry Carese accepted a high profile position as a Personal lines underwriter in the high net worth markets.

She strongly believes in health and wellness and does whatever she can to stay fit. Carese believes water is the best cleansing for the body and follows a strict diet. Her strong believes also afforded to strive in breaking the glass ceiling in Corporate America. Knowing that some will attempt to keep women and minorities from reaching the top, she has every intention of breaking that barrier. Her focus is attaining the success she knows she desires and will work hard for it. That attitude caused her drive and tenacious spirit to believe, "failure is not an option" and that the only person that can stop you from attaining your dreams and purpose in life, is YOU.

The QUEENDOM DIARIES
"pages from the diary of a queen"

Made in the USA
Columbia, SC
19 January 2019